Action research
handbook for
SOCIAL CHANGE
in Urban America

Action research handbook for SOCIAL CHANGE in Urban America

Mary Donahue
Boston University

James L. Spates
Hobart and William Smith Colleges

under the supervision of Max Birnbaum and John Mogey
Boston University

Harper & Row, Publishers
New York, Evanston, San Francisco, London

ACTION RESEARCH HANDBOOK FOR
SOCIAL CHANGE IN URBAN AMERICA

Standard Book Number: 06-040702-6

Library of Congress Catalog Card Number: 72-82163

To Morris Green and
the Joseph Fels Foundation

Contents

Preface

C. Wright Mills argued that personal problems when multiplied became public issues and sociology's subject matter. Sociology, composed of theoretical concepts and research reports, often seems removed from ordinary life. This handbook closes the distance between public or sociological issues and personal experience by giving the students an opportunity to use concepts in everyday settings. Much of the commentary, exercises, and suggestions for activities in this handbook were produced through the interaction of students and faculty in an experimental seminar taught at Boston University during several semesters. The seminars were supported in part by the Joseph Fels Foundation.

During the years 1968-1971, we assisted and taught an undergraduate seminar entitled Community and Social Change, that required each student to become involved in carrying out a field project. Many of our ideas and comments in this handbook are based on field projects completed for course requirements. We would like to acknowledge the special assistance and variety of ideas of the following Boston University students: Nancy Brudnick, Harvey Black, Sheila Rosenblum, Jerry Goldstein, Barbara Kleva, Anne Wilson, Karen Tucker, Joanne Kane, Helen Shedden, Yvonne Ramsey, Roberta Finkel, Andrea Steele, Barbara Brauner, Laurie Engel, Nancy Lerman, Ann Dargis, Clayton F. Bower, Jr., Deborah Cameron, Karl D. Klauck, Deborah N. Cutler, Anne Clark, Robert Paul Berish, Ann Swift, Jody Garber, Peter Francis, David Wluka, and Ellen Jane Gould.

This handbook is published together with a reader compiled by the authors' associates, Professors Max Birnbaum and John Mogey of the Boston University Sociology Department.

M. D.
J. L. S.

A Note to the Reader

This handbook is designed to accompany *Social Change in Urban America*, but it may also be used independently. It introduces the reader to the study of community on a personal basis. Believing that personal experiences dramatize and often amplify conventionally obtained knowledge, we suggest a variety of activities and exercises involving personal contact with actual community processes.

A community is a person's immediate social environment, the initial and often the most important resource for help. Today the community's public service bureaucracies are the main source of assistance for the individual. Thus in considering community operation, in both *Social Change in Urban America* and this handbook the focus is on the major public service bureaucracies in every community: education, police, and public welfare. Because they are found in all societies, these three services are a useful starting point in examining community operation. All communities today have formal organizations for socialization (education), social control (police), and social support (public welfare). Whether sophisticated or rudimentary, these public service bureaucracies affect all residents of the local community, either as direct recipients of the services or as indirect patrons through taxes and political support. Because of their universality, we assume that the reader has some familiarity with these services and their operation. Such previous experiences are beneficial as starting points for further learning.

We recommend two procedures in approaching the operation of communities or public service bureaucracies. The field experience is the most basic procedure, requiring a combination of personal encounters and reading on a topic to develop understanding. Fulfilling objectives as well as making additional discoveries render it a broad educational experience. Questioning and seeking information from various sources will bring unexpected encounters and important insights. Reflection on and evaluation of the expected and unexpected results of personal investigation comprise the learning process we call a field experience. Pulling together and interpreting these outcomes offer a vital and new understanding of the community and its operation.

The second procedure, the field project, consists of the investigation of a personally selected topic. One must devote all of one's resources to the project in order to profit intellectually and reach a successful completion. While field experience indicates the global way in which understanding of the subject matter can best be accomplished, a field project is more specifically based on an intensively examined aspect of community operation of particular interest.

In this handbook the study of community operation proceeds by detailing the nature and function of three major public service bureaucracies. While field experiences will occur for all of them, the field project is individually directed and limited to an aspect of just one.

Field projects have many possibilities. The public service bureaucracy defines an area of interest within which field projects can be developed. For example, focal aspects might be: social structure or social roles, recruitment and training procedures, social characteristics of employees or employers, or the public service bureaucracy's relationship to other social institutions.

Focusing on public service bureaucracies is useful because their complexity provides much variety in designing a field project. Since bureaucracies are functioning organizations, they influence community residents in many ways. The educational organization has contact not only with the community by educating its students, but also with the students' parents, taxpayers, and political decision makers. Many jobs in teaching, administration, and maintenance are available within the organization. These relationships enable the educational public service bureaucracy to interact with the community beyond its main focus on socialization. This interaction is also found in the other public service bureaucracies.

Before we proceed to outline the handbook's organization, it may be wise to issue a warning. Field experiences focus on dynamic situations in the social world. The subject matter of sociology comes from such social situations. The reader should recognize that although he is observing the same material as the professional sociologist, he is not yet equipped, by years of formal training, with the ability to produce sophisticated research results. The emphasis of a field experience is not on completing a formal sociological study but on using the opportunity to observe complex social phenomena. While we expect field projects to follow the basic ideas of social research, we do not expect them to use complex theories or methodologies. If the reader can take a few central sociological ideas and use them to understand the events happening in the lives of real people, he will advance his comprehension of the social world. The social world is so complex that in the short time of one semester we can only begin to build our sociological knowledge of it.

Success does not lie in a completed field project; in fact, it will probably raise more questions than it solves. Success occurs when the reader is satisfied that he has learned something about the real world, himself, or an aspect of life he has not previously known. To determine whether such learning takes place is something each person must decide for himself.

This handbook consists of six chapters. Chapter 1 provides background material to introduce the operation of field experiences and the construction of field projects. Section A of Chapter 1, Field Experience as a Procedure, introduces the concept of active field involvement. The broad concept of field experiences encompasses field projects as well as all additional and unexpected events contributing to the total impact of the educational experience. Section B, How to Carry Out a Field Project, gives practical suggestions on the most successful ways to construct and complete a field project. Since the basic ideas and procedures are essential to the approach of this handbook, Chapter 1 should be read several times.

As an introduction to the discussion of public service bureaucracies, Chapter 2—The Community, the Inner City, and the Bureaucracy—begins with sociological concepts drawn from *Social Change in Urban America* with which one must be familiar to approach a field experience with intellectual sophistication. In a series of concept clarification projects, the reader is asked to relate these concepts to one another to expand his understanding of their intricacies. Ways of using these concepts in developing field experiences are also suggested. A bibliography of additional readings completes the chapter.

Chapters 3 through 5 focus on three public service bureaucracies: Education (Chapter 3), Police (Chapter 4), and Public Welfare (Chapter 5). Each of these chapters begins by presenting concepts from the readings in *Social Change in Urban America* that are important to the bureaucracy under study. Concept clarification projects are suggested to interrelate and develop these ideas. Examples of field projects about the particular service under examination are discussed next. Providing a sampling of the potential variety of field projects, the examples are developed in three ways. First a detailed example of a possible field project is presented. Several additional projects for each bureaucracy are outlined for comparison. Finally, a list of subjects for field projects is included to indicate the great range of possible topics of study. These alternative projects have been successfully completed previously and are selected for their illustration of basic concepts and their design. A supplementary bibliography completes each chapter to serve as part of the sociological background literature for field projects.

Chapter 6 has directions for constructing field projects and provides space to design, refine, carry out, and interpret necessary procedures. The handbook concludes with an Appendix to be used as reference material. The first section not only considers basic methods, but also describes a series of techniques adapted from more rigorous sociological methodology. The discussion goes on to outline the rationale behind these procedures and concludes with a bibliography of suggested readings on research.

The last section of the Appendix considers how to apply this handbook to a rural environment. It suggests possibilities for field experiences and projects in rural settings and translates some of the fundamental issues and procedures previously discussed into concepts more appropriate to rural situations. This section is included in anticipation of the use of this handbook in institutions without easy access to metropolitan centers.

Action research handbook for SOCIAL CHANGE in Urban America

1

Introduction

A. FIELD EXPERIENCE AS A PROCEDURE

This handbook provides a detailed outline of how to design, conduct, and analyze field experiences in the social world. Field experiences grow out of projects that integrate actual encounters with people, agencies, and problems of the urban environment with sociological concepts and techniques. An indispensable part of learning about today's society, they are means by which readings about urban society are made meaningful through personal testing against reality. Field experiences allow one to see sociological concepts and processes operating in the real world. This emphasis makes possible the development of both theoretical knowledge about public service bureaucracies and actual direct contact with them, a combination essential to relevant education.

Although no prior experience with public service bureaucracies is necessary for successful field experiences, one must have a personal desire to learn something about the complexities of the social world. Through field experiences the individual defines what aspects of the social world are most relevant to him. By making contact with the social world, he learns what relation his studies and his own ideas have to reality. This contact is viewed within a research model to control against personal biases about the subject matter.

Under this analytic procedure the individual assumes responsibility for his own learning. Given a desire to learn he will work freely outside of class, researching and reading material that has not been assigned. Under these conditions he will contact people he has never met and go to unfamiliar places. Only by doing these things can one learn something personally valuable about how life is lived outside one's neighborhood, educational institution, or personal moral beliefs.

B. HOW TO CARRY OUT A FIELD PROJECT

This section discusses how to approach the steps of a field project. The real world, the focus of a field project, is complex and dynamic, and this makes planning difficult. The following steps suggest possibilities that might occur as one constructs, carries out, and analyzes a field project. At each step we have found certain procedures that are effective in making it easier and more meaningful, and they are outlined below.

1

The research steps and suggestions for success assume that the field project is a group effort, because of the multiplicity of tasks and questions involved. This is a matter of personal choice, however, and the following remarks are readily adaptable to individual projects.

1. Problem Formulation

In this first step one must decide on a general area to be studied and reduce it to manageable proportions. This can be done in two ways. The form for the written record of a field project in Chapter 6 contains a sequence of questions for each step. Answering these questions will reduce and specify the selected topic. Sharing one's ideas with others and receiving feedback will also narrow the initial topic and introduce new perspectives.

Natural focusing is not easy or spontaneous, but there are other alternatives. Consideration of basic objectives may make the focus appear more sharply.

Once the focus of the field project is specifically defined, the problem must be shaped into manageable proportions. This task is more difficult than selecting a topic. Most people will have had little prior experience with field studies and will tend to take on too much in beginning the project. Failing to realize how short a college term is, they will set up analyses that would take too long to complete. To avoid this error, the student should remember that the purpose of a field project is not to produce sophisticated research but rather to understand some of the processes of the social world by confronting that world as a fledgling sociologist. Because social practices are complex, simplicity is the most important word to remember in planning a field project.

The process of narrowing a topic continues by discussing and evaluating areas that are important to analyze for understanding the problem. The reader should begin to apply sociological knowledge gained from the readings in *Social Change in Urban America*. Narrowing is also helped by continued reading in the area under consideration and introducing sociological concepts that clarify prior work done in the selected area. This refining process should reveal a definite focus for the field project.

When the topic of the field project is clearly formulated, its manageability in terms of time and resources should be considered. This should be done in a specific manner, considering together the tentative outline, the time available for work on each segment of the field project, the resources available, the library facilities, and the potential contacts. Once these factors have been evaluated, the final statement of the field project can be drafted.

2. Hypothesis Formulation

After the topic has been defined it should be put into hypothetical form, if possible. If the topic is of an exploratory nature one cannot hypothesize about it. In this case the nature and extent of the issue should be clearly stated. In its conclusion, an exploratory field project will yield a hypothesis, such as a statement about what influences are causing or are associated with the specific issue or problem being studied. Because of the earlier attempts to define the topic a clear statement of the hypothesis of the research problem should be readily completed. If it does not appear, it is a sign that the narrowing-down process has not been detailed enough.

3. Data Collection

Once the problem is clearly stated, data are collected in order to decide how the problem is to be measured. Measurement requires selecting a research technique appropriate to the problem and designing a method of revealing the variables under investigation.

Data collection should be well organized and proceed according to a previously established plan. Problems are likely to arise, and possible solutions should be thought out in advance. Anticipating potential obstacles helps prevent slowdowns and stoppages in data collection. During the actual data collection the researchers should stay in close contact with one another, since adequate communication will facilitate quick handling of any problem that might arise.

4. Analysis

The analytical phase of the field project has three sections: initial inspection of the data, making a decision about the hypothesis or understanding the problem explored, and summarizing results of the research. Initial data analysis involves preliminary inspection of the results that suggest the orientation of the final conclusions.

The decision as to whether the data do or do not support the hypotheses can be fairly automatic. Although there is often an observable trend, the decision will not be obvious when there are contradictions in the data. In these cases the data must be reported as mixed, and one should discuss the results and evaluate possible reasons for such outcomes.

The third phase of analysis, comparison of the results of the field project with previous findings, leads to considering the implications of the outcomes for the area under study, for the people studied, and for sociology as a whole. This is an important summing-up phase that may suggest additional questions, hypotheses, and problems.

5. Reporting

Overall evaluation of the field project and its outcomes leads directly to reporting on both a personal and a group level. A procedure for handling individual reports is contained in Chapter 6.

Preliminary discussions and oral presentations are helpful in drafting the written report. Exchanging and challenging ideas reveal new interpretations and conclusions. Oral presentation allows one to develop and organize the outcomes of the field project before finalizing them in a final report and gives others a different set of perspectives with which to reconsider their own projects.

The final written report may be handled in one of several ways. One way is to have the report written by one or two members of the group with the other members serving as input resources by supplying the necessary information in organized fashion.

A second approach has each member of the group writing a section of the final report. One would write the introductory and problem formulation material, another the hypothesis and data collection phase, and the third the data analysis and conclusions. This procedure allows each member to get involved in some section of the field project, but it does not produce a consistent perspective on the problem.

A third alternative has each member write his own version of the study. This method produces shorter reports than if the field project were written up collectively. It allows each member to write about what was important to him and also provides each member a chance to compare his perspective on the field project with the other perspectives.

This concludes our discussion of guidelines useful in carrying out a field project. They can be supplemented by three suggestions. First, discuss at length the problems that are under consideration. Second, if resolution on a specific topic eludes you, take the problem to the instructor. His experience with field projects makes it easier for him to see and resolve the difficulties. Third, if these alternatives fail, take the problem to the whole class. The added number of interested minds should solve the difficulties.

A field project, coupled with sociological material, can be a very rewarding experience in one's education. In constructing, carrying out, and analyzing a field project, one must remember to define success in personal terms, never wholly in academic terms. It does not matter that a field project works out in a way you never expected. The real learning value may lie in discovering the reasons for the unexpected results.

2

The community, the inner city, and the bureaucracy

A. INTRODUCTION

This handbook examines education, police, and public welfare in their relationship to the inner city. Today these bureaucracies, present in some form in every community, are under stress and face criticism. This chapter aims to show why this situation exists before considering (in Chapters 3, 4, and 5) the activities and trouble spots in these bureaucracies.

We must first understand what bureaucracies are and how they relate to local communities. This chapter explains and develops concepts of community and bureaucracy and presents essential topics concerning their current problems. Also included are discussions of urbanism, inner city, lifestyle, and ideology. Understanding the meaning of these concepts helps the investigation of today's widely reported bureaucratic and community stress.

B. CONCEPTS

1. Community

The concept of community calls to mind the stereotype of the small rural American town, the ideal of democratic society. A community is a mutually interdependent group of people, basically homogeneous in social characteristics, who live in a fairly well-defined geographic area and whose shared social life provides virtually all of life's basic necessities. The concept of community has been widely applied in another sense. In this era of seeking real or pretended attachments, we often see references to the "community" of scholars, dog-lovers, or musicians. These usages are based on the homogeniety component of the given definition and overlook the territorial referent.

More accurately community refers to the group's self-consciousness of living together and sharing a common fate. In terms of a quantitative basis, a community can provide all services necessary to insure its inhabitants a complete life. This definition emphasizes a community's potential for allowing the living of a complete life within it. A community offers the minimal necessities for sustaining an individual's entire life; it includes—at least in rudimentary form—education, food, health care, jobs, and recreation. People could theoretically live out an entire life within the confines of an area like the Addams area described by Suttles (1969). Most people choose not to exist within just one community.

There are two basic constituents of a community. The first is a commonly held set of emotional ties between a group which generates a mutually shared identification. The community's emotional bond links all members together on a seemingly egalitarian basis; all are members of that community. The emotional bond creates interest in and concern for the community; because people feel for the community, they care what happens to it. Their own self-identity merges in a small way with the identity of the community. The second constituent is a territorial referent; the community must be located in space and time and have fairly well-defined boundaries to distinguish members from nonmembers. A community must have some type of limits or boundaries. Territorial definitions are the most immediate and easily definable. Boundaries heighten emotional ties because members and nonmembers are clearly set apart. The territorial basis of community was more clearly specified when communities were isolated and agrarian. With industrialization and the separation of the home and workplace, there are more ambiguities in defining community boundaries. Boundaries retain their function to distinguish members from nonmembers.

2. Urbanism

Many types of communities have been described—farm communities, manufacturing communities, business and financial communities, residential communities—but basically communities can be considered as predominantly rural or urban. Rural communities existed historically prior to urban communities. They are organized around agriculture and farming and are smaller in size than urban communities. Urban communities appear with the specialization of tasks and the rise of industrialism. Home and workplace are separated. Urban characteristics reflect this specialization of tasks. Urban communities generally have clearly marked business areas as well as slums, manufacturing districts, areas of working-class homes, and suburban residential areas.

No community is either completely rural or urban; we employ these categories as ideal types. Ideal types provide exaggerated examples or abstractions against which we can measure real communities. We say that one community is more rural than another by drawing on our ideal type of total rural life, which is self-sufficient, isolated, and mainly agricultural.

Urbanization refers to the process by which a community becomes less rural and more specialized. Urbanization means the simultaneous occurrence of many things; separation of home and workplace, specialization of tasks, increased division of labor, increased prevalence of smaller nuclear family structures, and increased emphasis on formal education. The process of urbanization heightens the efficiency and speed of societal operation and is likely to occur when the increased size of the population demands more efficient production and distribution of goods and communication.

Urbanization generates a condition of society called urbanism. Wirth (1938) states that size, density, and heterogeniety create urbanism. Increased size (greater numbers of people) makes intensely personal social life impossible. People lack the pyschological energy to interact warmly with the thousands of people encountered daily in a modern city. Size, combined with the high density characteristic of cities, puts necessary limitations on the content of much of social life for purely self-protective reasons.

Urbanism is associated with impersonalized social contacts and segmented social roles. People react to each other according to what the other does or is in terms of labels, rather than in terms of the whole person with his unique set of talents, limitations, personality, and idiosyncracies. The size and density of city life create this limit on emotional response. Urbanism further promotes a reserved, detached, so-called sophisticated demeanor among its inhabitants. This reserve often verges onto callousness when an accident or crime occurs and the bystanders ignore it for fear of involvement. The injured person is not known as a person and, without emotional involvement, it is easy to dismiss the tragedy from one's mind and one's sense of responsibility.

Heterogeniety, another component of urbanism, means that cities are composed of different types of people doing different things. City-dwellers have many occupations, religions, races, socio-economic positions, and interests. Cities promote heterogeniety by providing outlets and opportunities for diverse interests and capabilities. The complexity and attractiveness of cities spring from this diverse intermingling. By contrast a farming village lacks a range of possibilities; its inhabitants have relatively similar occupations, religions, interests, and socio-economic positions. Cities offer many possibilities, while more homogeneous communities provide fewer options.

The urban community encompasses a multitude of lifestyles, values, and jobs. People living in cities can find others who share similar unusual sets of aims and activities. Cities have areas composed of white slums, black ghettos, transients in boarding houses, young families, and ethnic groups. Within the diversity of the city, people select an area and define a lifestyle most appropriate to their resources and ambitions.

3. The Inner City

Within cities we find many types of communities: slums, ghettos, bohemian and art colonies, skid rows, actors' enclaves, working-class residences. These areas, which are generally situated around the city's central business district, are collectively categorized as the inner city. The inner city includes people existing in lower socio-economic positions and who live in the most inexpensive locations in our communities, either due to economics, discrimination, or by choice. Inner-city residents usually possess little or none of the assets valued by the larger society: occupational skills, education, income, and white skin.

Cities are entry points for newcomers to society, whether from rural farms or foreign lands, and the inner city is the place within the city where they arrive. The inner city's composition has two forms, one of which is a channel for immigrating ethnic groups and displaced migrating rural residents, and these minorities form cohesive insular groups. While occupying a marginal position with relation to the value structure of the larger community, they maintain many of their former ways in their new setting. Suttles (1969) and Gans (1962) illustrate the internal coherence of such groups' moral codes and value systems, which appear mysterious and amoral to the outsider. Despite their disorganized appearance, these newcomers frequently have formed tight networks and ties.

The inner city has been known for many years. Early immigrants called it a ghetto. Since 1950 and the postwar rural migration from the South when black Americans became the dominant ethnic group, it has become a racial ghetto. Racism adds a special twist to the contemporary inner city. The essential features are visibly intensified, but the basic forces remain the same.

Counting black Americans separately is a sign of racial concern. After one generation is born in America, Irish, Jewish, Italian, Polish, and other Europeans count as native-born white Americans. In spite of 350 years—ten generations of American births, the black man is still counted as nonwhite. Racial prejudice is a main reason for the concentration of black Americans in the inner city, because nowhere else can they get housing. Black Americans are far more affected by this prejudice than are Chinese, Puerto Ricans, or Mexican Americans.

Personal offenses, robbery in the streets, fights, murders, and other crimes are much more frequent in the inner city than in middle-income areas. A small number of active purse-snatchers, robbers that prowl continuously, and specialized burglars generate a high rate of crime. Since the victims are their neighbors who are poor like themselves, they must make many hold-ups in order to profit. The poor rob the poor and the blacks rob the blacks, not from choice but simply as a matter of convenience.

The inner city is a threat to life and property because of overcrowding, lack of garbage collection, abandoned buildings, and the use of the streets for business—all of which produce a dangerous physical environment. Fires in abandoned buildings, overcrowded tenements, dirty and small-scale factories, the noise of traffic, abandoned automobiles on the side streets, and the stench of garbage, make the inner city an undesirable place to live. The infestation of rats, cockroaches, lice, and fleas in houses and on the streets is a major condition for epidemics.

The inner city has a second form: a receptacle for people minimally attached to the dominant societal values. It captures people whose socio-economic position is downwardly mobile, such as the elderly. It also contains those who choose to operate outside conventional occupational and status structures, such as the purveyors of illicit activities, hippies, and transients. These people have either rejected the values of the larger society or are rejected by these values. The hippy and the criminal prefer to act outside society's normative structure, while the elderly are downwardly mobile because they possess neither economic resources nor potential for maintaining themselves in a cleaner and less-troubled environment.

Life in the inner city lacks personal networks between and emotional ties to life in surrounding areas. The outsider's perception of the area's social structure as amorphous and random captures the transiency and immediacy of inner-city lives. The inner city combines two extremes: (1) community cohesiveness, extremely close networks based on parochial values, and (2) transients, deviants, criminals, and others outside the established normative patterns of the larger society. However, despite the diversity of social organizations and value systems coexisting within the inner-city area, it is uniformly filled with suffering and misery. Inner-city residents are worse off than other people on most measures— they work longer hours, get dirtier, earn less money, have less job security, are ill more often, suffer more mental illness, have more divorces, experience less marital satisfaction, and have more poorly developed parent-child relationships. Painfully aware of their situation, they are by and large made even more miserable by knowing that other people have a low opinion of them as well.

4. Lifestyle

People living adjacent to inner-city areas are immediately aware of the poverty and misery nearby, but this initial evaluation is superficial. As we have mentioned, the inner city is created and maintained by several different categories of people. These categories indicate that similar behavioral manifestations and physical conditions represent different lifestyles. The meaning imputed by inner-city residents to certain dimensions of life may be very different from that imputed to the same thing by the outside observer. Overcrowding and poor housing conditions are often positively defined as supportive and overlaid with socially derived meanings. Gans (1962) discusses the rich social life of Boston's West End residents that occured within substandard housing and densely inhabited neighborhoods. Physical reality is interpreted by social categories, and these must be more carefully considered.

The concept of lifestyle refers to patterns of acting and thinking defined by certain symbolic systems and employed by distinct groups of people. To the outside observer, inner-city behavior may appear hedonistic, immediate, and amoral. This misinterpretation is based on an ignorance of values and intent.

Rustin (1966) shows that the frequent reports of unrestrained violence in the Watts riot of 1965 were misleading. Observers of these events were not familiar with the orientation of the inner-city residents' lifestyle. Common sense interpretations are not enough to capture the meanings the actions had for the riot participants. Violence occurred selectively and symbolically. The riots indicated the onset of the Watts residents' realization that they could assert themselves and be listened to within the larger society (Rustin, 1966). Any attempt to study communities, inner-city areas, and the operation of bureaucracies should include an understanding of the symbolic content of the inhabitants' lifestyles.

5. Bureaucracy

Gerth and Mills' (1958) excerpts from Weber's works offer the most precise definition of a bureaucracy. A bureaucracy is an organization oriented toward rationality and efficiency in producing things. Bureaucracies hire people on their qualifications to perform definite tasks and promotion and reward are determined by merit. In order to have tasks completed in the fastest, most efficient, and cheapest manner, they endeavor to exclude all personal and emotional components. Because bureaucracies are organized on strictly rational lines, personal requests are categorized and established procedures are laid down so that response to them is impersonal.

Authority and responsibility in a bureaucracy are hierarchical, each worker occupying a particular niche with its own clearly defined realm of responsibility. A few individuals set the overall policy, work out the exact chain of command, and decide precisely the limits of authority inherent in every position within the hierarchy. Each employee must cooperate with the persons above and below him so that the bureaucracy's objectives can be fulfilled.

Bureaucracies represent the most efficient way to handle and expedite masses of material because they ignore the personal element. Once an issue is categorized, the appropriate answer or outcome can be delivered. The appearance of bureaucracies is the inevitable outcome of the size and diversity of cities. The need for immediate and simultaneous provision of many types of service requires a regular, rational, and predictable mechanism of distribution. As an organizing device, bureaucracies replace informal provisions of service dependent on personal contacts and kin networks, as in more homogeneous communities. With increased size and demands, purely rational procedures such as bureaucracies were developed to provide adequate and fast distribution to many people.

There are many types of bureaucracies, for example, the United States Army, Boston University, the Roman Catholic Church, the New York City Police Department, the International Business Machine Corporation, and the Family Service Association of America. The same characteristics— rationality, valuing efficiency, formal qualification for job assignment—apply to them all.

Bureaucracies also have clients, which are the people or organizations whom the bureaucracy supplies with a service to help with specific problems. When a bureaucracy's client is another bureaucracy, clashes and misunderstandings are reduced because they understand each other's procedures. When the client is not a bureaucracy but is more personal and less rational, communication problems arise. For example, the basic principles of bureaucracies and communities diverge. When a community is the client of a bureaucracy there will be difficulties, because a bureaucracy values rationality, while a community appreciates affective, personal ties. Community satisfaction with the operation of the bureaucracies of police, education, and public welfare depends on the existence of effective mechanisms for communication of needs and responses between a community and the bureaucracies trying to serve it.

When communities lack personal networks and political spokesmen, bureaucracies such as the police operate without the guidance and restraint of community influence and opinion. Community members react to the communication void by perceiving the bureaucracy as heartless and inconsiderate. Unaware that a community exists, the bureaucracy sees its clients as disorganized masses of irresponsible individuals. Clients perceive the bureaucracy as doing a good job when it meets their subjectively defined needs as communicated by political spokesmen and personal networks.

At the other extreme, very tightly knit communities, such as ethnic communities, have no real need for bureaucratic provision of services. So strong are their personal networks that all subjectively perceived needs are satisfied through them. Here bureaucracies constitute a second level of service provision, an imposition on a community. In both cases there are no effective channels for communication with the bureaucracy operating in these situations. Without communication there can be no exchange and no correction of faulty perceptions and messages. Even if there is effective communication between a community and the bureaucracies assigned to serve it, basic differences between them hinder completing service of all needs and perfect satisfaction with the provision.

Bureaucratic employees are middle class people because they have the necessary level of education to effectively carry out the required tasks. When bureaucracies such as police, welfare, and education deal with inner-city residents and their problems, social class differences create communication barriers and a lack of mutual understanding that impede the effectiveness of their ameliorative attempts.

6. Ideology

Bureaucratic employees develop their own set of concepts to interpret clients' messages and lifestyles. Boesel et al. (1969) use the term *ideology* to convey the complex of irrationalities and inconsistencies that bureaucratic employees working in inner-city areas use to interpret the lifestyles of inner-city residents. Teachers in the inner city made the inconsistent observation that education is a most important asset, but that inner-city students were unable to learn.

Bureaucratic agents often deny the causative role of social forces and enunciate some version of the "Negro disability thesis" (Boesel et al, 1969). They want to believe that problems lie within individuals rather than being consequences of intolerable social situations. By its nature an ideology is composed of psychologically irrational elements, functioning as a set of blinders to allow bureaucratic employees to continue their assigned tasks despite the enormity of the very apparent problems surrounding them.

C. CONCEPT CLARIFICATION PROJECTS

We have discussed six concepts basic to mastery of the material in this handbook. This descriptive material provides a background for explaining and interrelating your ideas. In this section you can display your familiarity with and understanding of the concepts in Section B. In answering these items, draw on your personal experiences and insights in light of the material you have read.

Questions Requiring Short Paragraph Answers

1. a. Define the community in which you grew up.
    b. What are its boundaries? Does it have any sense of having outsiders in it?
    c. What kinds of personal contacts does it have?
    d. Do you have difficulty applying the concept of community? If so, why?
    e. Select another area you feel is a community according to the definition given above, and tell why it is a community.
    f. Select another community (if you chose an urban community above, select a rural community now, and vice versa) and compare and contrast the two. Why is one urban and the other rural, and what are their distinguishing characteristics?
    g. Select another area and explain why it is not a community.

2. a. Give at least three examples of the urbanization processes you have experienced. What characteristics of urbanization do they demonstrate?
    b. From your own experience describe the characteristics of city life. Can you think of things commonly seen in cities that contradict Wirth's (1938) characteristics of urbanism, size, density, and heterogeneity?
    c. Describe some people you know who live the way of life known as urbanism.
    d. Select an urban community that you feel can be called a city. Using the definition given above, why is it a city? How does it fit or not fit?

3. a. Give an example of an inner city. How do you distinguish it from other areas of the city?
    b. What is the relationship of the inner city to the rest of the city or the community?
    c. Does every city or community have an inner-city area? Why?

4. a. It is commonly believed that you can never really know anything from a distance; that true knowledge comes from participation. How does this statement relate to the concept of lifestyle?
    b. Why are many reports on inner-city conditions misleading?

5. a. Are bureaucracies an important social invention, as Max Weber contended? Why?
    b. Make a list of ten bureaucracies not mentioned here.
    c. What are some ways in which public service bureaucracies differ from other bureaucracies?

6. a. Why do ideologies arise? What could help to lessen them?
    b. What harm do ideologies do? Do they perform any good function?

Summary Questions

The following topics require more detailed answers. Think carefully about the many possible meanings involved in each one, and try to include many aspects of the issue you are considering. Use readings and personal observations.

1. Do the characteristics of urbanism diminish the possibility of community?

2. What are the attitudes of the community toward inner-city residents?

3. What is the nature of the interrelationships between bureaucracies and people?

4. What are the consequences of lifestyle for communication? Consider the situation of the inner-city resident and the operation of bureaucracies.

5. What is the relationship between the socio-economic backgrounds of bureaucratic employees and their manifestations of ideological viewpoints about inner-city lifestyles?

D. SUPPLEMENTARY BIBLIOGRAPHY

Agger, Robert E., Daniel Goldrich, and Bert Swanson.
    1964   *The Rulers and the Ruled.* New York: Wiley.
Banfield, Edward C.
    1970   *The Unheavenly City.* Boston: Little, Brown.
Banfield, Edward C., and James Q. Wilson.
    1963   *City Politics.* Cambridge: Harvard University Press.
Becker, Howard (ed.).
    1967   *Social Problems.* New York: Wiley.
Boesel, David, et al.
    1969   "White institutions and black rage." *Trans*-action 6 (March): 24-31.
Bruyn, Severyn T.
    1963   *Communities In Action.* New Haven: College and University Press.
Clark, Kenneth B.
    1965   *Dark Ghetto.* New York: Harper & Row.
Clark, Kenneth B., and Jeannette Hopkins.
    1968   *A Relevant War Against Poverty: A Study of Community Action Programs and Observable Social Change.* New York: Harper & Row.
Coleman, James.
    1957   *Community Conflict.* New York: Free Press.
Conot, Robert.
    1967   *Rivers of Blood, Years of Darkness.* New York: Bantam.
Drake, St. Clair and Horace Cayton.
    1962   *Black Metropolis,* 2 vol. New York: Harcourt Brace Jovanovich.
Duhl, Leonard (ed.).
    1963   *The Urban Condition.* New York: Basic Books.
Etzioni, Amitai (ed.).
    1969   *The Semi-Professions and Their Organization: Teachers, Nurses and Social Workers.* New York: Free Press.
Form, William H. and Delbert Miller.
    1960   *Industry, Labor and Community.* New York: Harper & Row.
Gans, Herbert.
    1962   *The Urban Villagers.* New York: Free Press.
Gerth, Hans, and C. Wright Mills (eds.).
    1958   *From Max Weber: Essays in Sociology.* New York: Oxford University Press.

Gitlin, Todd, and Nanci Hollander.
    1970   *Uptown.* New York: Harper & Row.
Glazer, Nathan, and Daniel Moynihan.
    1963   *Beyond the Melting Pot.* Cambridge: M.I.T. Press.
Gordon, Mitchell.
    1966   *Sick Cities.* Baltimore: Penguin.
Hammer, Richard.
    1964   "Report from a Spanish Harlem fortress." *New York Times Magazine* (July 5).
Harrington, Michael.
    1962   *The Other America.* Baltimore: Penguin.
HARYOU-ACT.
    1964   *Youth in the Ghetto.* New York: Haryou.
Jacobs, Jane.
    1961   *The Death and Life of Great American Cities.* New York: Random House.
Jacobs, Paul
    1967   *Prelude to Riot: A View of Urban America from the Bottom.* New York: Random House.
Katz, F. E.
    1966   "Social participation and social structure." *Social Forces* 45 (December): 199-210.
Koenig, Rene.
    1968   *The Community.* New York: Humanities.
Liebow, Elliot.
    1967   *Tally's Corner.* Boston: Little, Brown.
Lowry, Nelson, C. E. Ramsey, and C. Verner.
    1960   *Community Structure and Change.* New York: Macmillan.
Lyford, Joseph.
    1966   *The Air-Tight Cage.* New York: Harper & Row.
Martin, Roscoe, et al.
    1961   *Decisions in Syracuse.* Garden City, N.Y.: Doubleday.
Marx, Gary T.
    1967   *Protest and Prejudice: A Study of Belief in the Black Community.* New York: Harper & Row.
Miller, S. M., and Frank Riessman.
    1968   *Social Class and Social Policy.* New York: Basic Books.
Morris, Robert (ed.).
    1964   *Centrally Planned Change.* New York: National Association of Social Workers.
Moynihan, Daniel P.
    1968   "The professors and the poor." *Commentary* 46 (August): 3-11.
Osofosky, Gilbert.
    1968   *Harlem: the Making of a Ghetto.* New York: Harper & Row.
Park, Robert E., and Ernest W. Burgess.
    1925   *The City.* Chicago: University of Chicago Press.
Parsons, Talcott, and Kenneth B. Clark (eds.).
    1966   *The Negro American.* Boston: Houghton Mifflin.
Riis, Jacob.
    1957   *How the Other Half Lives.* New York: Hill & Wang.
Rustin, Bayard.
    1966   "The Watts 'manifesto' and the McCone report." *Commentary* 41 (March): 29-35.
Ryan, William.
    1971   *Blaming the Victim.* New York: Pantheon.

Schnore, Leo T. (ed.).
    1967   *Social Science and the City: A Survey of Urban Research.* New York: Praeger.
Seeley, John.
    1959   "The slum: its nature, use and users." *Journal of the American Institute of Planners* 25 (February):7-14.
Silberman, Charles.
    1964   *Crisis in Black and White.* New York: Random House.
Skolnick, Jerome.
    1969   *The Politics of Protest.* New York: Ballantine.
Smythe, Hugh H., and James A. Moss.
    1963   "Human relations among the culturally deprived." *Journal of Human Relations* 13:524-537.
Suttles, Gerald.
    1969   "Anatomy of a Chicago slum." *Trans*-action 4:16-25.
Trans-action.
    1969   "The American under-class." *Trans*-action 6 (February): whole issue.
Valentine, Charles.
    1968   *Culture and Poverty: Critique and Counter-Proposals.* Chicago: University of Chicago Press.
Vidich, Arthur J., and J. Bensman.
    1958   *Small Town in Mass Society.* Garden City, N.Y.: Doubleday.
Warren, Roland.
    1963   *The Community in America.* Skokie, Ill.: Rand McNally.
Wheeler, Harvey.
    1968   "A moral equivalent for riots." *Saturday Review* (May 11):19-22, 51-52.
Wilensky, Harold.
    1964   "The professionalization of everyone." *American Journal of Sociology* 70 (September):137-158.
Wilkins, Leslie.
    1965   *Social Deviance: Social Policy, Action, and Research.* Englewood Cliffs, N.J.: Prentice-Hall.
Williams, Robin.
    1964   *Strangers Next Door.* Englewood Cliffs, N.J.: Prentice-Hall.
Wirth, Louis.
    1928   *The Ghetto.* Chicago: University of Chicago Press.
    1938   "Urbanism as a way of life." *American Journal of Sociology* 34 (July):1-24.
Wright, Nathan.
    1968a   *Black Power and Urban Unrest: Creative Possibilities.* New York: Hawthorn.
    1968b   *Ready to Riot.* New York: Holt, Rinehart & Winston.
Zorbaugh, Harvey.
    1929   *The Gold Coast and the Slum.* Chicago: University of Chicago Press.

3

Education

A. INTRODUCTION

In Chapter 3 we discuss public schools, which constitute the basis of the educational public service bureaucracy. Section B presents sociological concepts drawn from the readings in *Social Change in Urban America* that help to clarify the sociological aspects of education and give ideas of the applicability of these concepts. In Section C a set of Concept Clarification Projects uses these sociological concepts to think about education. The exercises in this section provide opportunities to explore the sociological aspects of schools.

Section D includes a variety of field projects on education, drawn from projects actually completed. There are three subsections. The first one, A Detailed Example of an Educational Field Project, is a precise chronological narrative of the procedure followed in developing the particular described project. This discussion includes many aspects of project development, topic selecting, conceptual refining, confronting obstacles, redesigning as necessary, and interpreting contradictory outcomes. Its value lies in the candid nature of the presentation, showing the myriad decisions, revisions, and flexibility, necessary in social research.

The second subsection, Other Examples of Educational Field Projects, presents briefer accounts of five field projects. Here we also try to convey in a more condensed manner the evolution of a field project, and also show some of the variety of topics and techniques possible. The third subsection, Suggestions for Field Projects, lists possible topics for field projects on education. This list is only a beginning; the individual's interests, opinions, and experiences can add to it.

The final section, Section E, is a supplementary bibliography on education, a reference source for material on topics of interest. It is not inclusive but is composed of items we have found useful in our experience.

B. CONCEPTS

1. Social System

System is a common scientific term drawn from the natural or physical sciences. A system is composed of interrelated and interdependent items. An example would be a functioning automobile engine. You can not remove the sparkplugs and have the engine continue to operate, because all the parts are interdependent.

The operating engine requires the presence of all its constituent parts, and removal or damage to any one part impairs or even prevents the engine's operation. Interdependency is the most essential characteristic of a system.

The solar system is another example of a system. It is an interrelated set of bodies consisting of satellites of the sun which are interdependent because of their gravitational pull on each other. We could not remove one of the satellites without destroying the solar system as we know it; a new solar system would automatically be formed.

We are very familiar with systems in physical sciences and mechanics. But the system of most interest to us is the social system, formed by human beings through continuing contacts in social roles. A social system is a set of two or more people playing complementary roles with a defined relationship to one another. Two people talking to each other as friends is an example of a social system, the talk being the way they are interrelated to one another. If one person leaves, what happens to the conversational exchange of friends? The person remaining is no longer part of that social system, and his actions must change. The two-person social system of friends is gone.

We form social systems when we contact other human beings as members of shared and predictable role sets. We adjust our behavior to that of the other person, and, when the other leaves, we must readjust our behavior to his absence.

Social systems are usually more complex than just two friends conversing. The school classroom is a larger social system. Each person acts as either a student or teacher and is interdependent with every other person. If we removed the teacher from the classroom, there would be different behavior among the remaining persons. The social system of the school classroom would dissolve and the social system of friends might appear. Every time a person enters or leaves the classroom, the social system changes.

There are also large, complex social systems encompassing many smaller subsystems. Groups of classrooms comprise the social system of the school. Groups of schools are school systems, generally one to a community, and all the local school systems together are the educational system.

The concept of social system is important in sociology and is used to discuss the public service bureaucracies. The sociologist looks at different social systems to compare and contrast them one with another. Understanding and using the concept of social system helps analyze social phenomena and differentiates between aspects of social life.

2. The School System and Socialization

The school system formally instructs new entrants how to become members of society and, by a selection process, allocates them to certain positions within the society. It generates motivation within society's new members appropriate to the roles played. All societies have specific ways of introducing and enforcing their own rules. This instruction insures a flow of people who accept the society's values and perform the tasks necessary for the society's maintenance. This process of social instruction is known as *socialization*.

There are two types of socialization: formal and informal. Occurring most frequently in the home among parents and young children, informal socialization also takes place in work situations and, to some degree, in all social settings. This is not education in the strict sense. Education is formal socialization in that it follows a set of procedures and is conducted by an organization whose function it is to instruct people. It helps new society members develop their potential and gives them the necessary knowledge to act in different situations. Formal socialization is selective, emphasizing certain behavior and ideas and deemphasizing others.

3. The School Classroom and Values

The classroom is the school's basic unit, being the place in which most formal socialization occurs. The school classroom handles socialization by developing individual intellectual capacities and teaching those commitments necessary for becoming a full-fledged member of society. The latter is done by instructing directly and indirectly society's values.

Values are ideas held by men as guidelines for behavior and as criteria by which men judge whether actions are good or bad. There are two levels of values: cultural and ethnic. Cultural values are shared by all members of the society and agreed upon as legitimate goals to strive for in life. Achievement, rationality, and economic wealth are values widespread in American society.

People are not continually aware of the influence of values. Internal, often unconscious, attachment to values guides behavior. It is this subtle, yet predominant, attachment to overriding ideas that we call commitment to the basic values of the society. It is the task of the schools to ensure that these cultural values are impressed on all members of the society.

There is never total agreement on all the cultural or general values of a society. Shared values are recognized by all members of society as socially legitimate goals. There is great diversity within any society because people choose to emphasize one value and ignore others. While an artist may renounce the value of economic wealth for himself, he recognizes that economic prosperity is a value held by others in the society.

Ethnic values are not shared by all members of the society but are unique to a particular subculture. They are important in specific situations, for example, where a group of a particular race, color, or creed dominates the schools. Ethnic values are taught indirectly, and this is the most important way they are transmitted. A teacher may be an Italian-American in a predominantly Italian-American community and unconsciously emphasize her own ethnic values and outlook on life. She undeliberately reinforces Italian-American attitudes about current affairs and ways of life. This is tolerable when there is harmony of backgrounds between the teacher and her pupils.

Conflicts between ethnic values arise, for example, when there is an Italian-American teacher in a predominantly black neighborhood school, or a Roman Catholic teacher in a school in a largely Jewish neighborhood. Today's schools are having important confrontations concerning which values should predominate. The question arises, as Birnbaum (1964) points out, of whose ethnic values should be taught? Should they reflect the values of the dominant group or of one minority or another? Many school systems face heavy criticism on this issue. Many communities, both of blacks, of ethnics, and of unique religious groups, argue that their children have a right to be taught their own history and heritage and not just a middle-class outlook. This conflict about the place of subcultures is an important issue of our time.

4. Definition of the Situation
and the Self-Fulfilling Prophecy

Some time ago an American sociologist, W. I. Thomas, developed a theorem called the *definition of the situation* that became very useful in sociology and of special interest in analyzing schools. He said that if men define situations as real, they are real in their consequences. Each man sees the social world in his own way: as he sees it, he defines it; and as he defines it, that definition becomes real. The definition comes into existence for him because he acts in terms of it.

The definition of the situation happens continually in social life. We define various situations, and by doing so, we make those situations real and must deal with the new reality. A teacher's reaction to a pupil's learning problem reflects the definition of the situation. The teacher may see a pupil having difficulty reading and conclude that he needs to have his eyes checked. This is one definition of the situation. Another teacher observing the same pupil might conclude differently that the boy is a slow learner and needs to be placed in a remedial class. This second definition of the situation is far more fateful, a decision that could shape the rest of the boy's life. Even if the second definition was objectively wrong, it would have real consequences. It would be acted on as if it were true and would create its own set of consequences. The boy placed in a remedial class would in time see himself as a slow learner. It would only be a matter of time until he became one.

The consequence of a false definition of the situation has another sociological term, the *self-fulfilling prophecy*. Robert Merton defines the self-fulfilling prophecy as a false definition of the situation evoking a new behavior which makes the originally false conception true. The classic example of the self-fulfilling prophecy is the student with a great fear of failing examinations. This fear is his definition of the situation. Obviously it is not a correct definition, for if he studies, he will pass the examination. But having made his decision, the student worries about the coming examination, studies little, and consequently fails. He fulfilled his own false prophesy for himself. He defined the situation incorrectly, acted in terms of the definition, and made the consequence come true.

Fuchs' (1968) article is an example of the same process. This article presents the situation of the new teacher in a ghetto school. Initially the teacher feels that she can help the children grow and learn. The task proved harder than expected and the teacher had little success. At first she thought the problem might be with herself, with her inability to grasp the situation correctly, her inability to give the children what they need. But this is an upsetting definition of the situation to hold because it puts the blame on the teacher. In time the teacher begins to believe the other teachers that it is the fault of the pupils who do not want to learn and their homes which do not equip them with the intellectual tools for learning, rather than the teacher's or the school's fault. The teacher divides her class into "good" students and "bad" students and finds that the "good" students did well and the "bad" ones poorly (Fuchs, 1968).

Many things happen in social life based on false definitions of the situation or self-fulfilling prophesies. But in actual social situations where self-fulfilling prophesies are at work, it is not easy to detect the incorrect definition because social life is so complex.

Another example of two definitions of the situation is contained in the exchange of articles by Alsop (1967a and 1967b) and Schwartz, Pettigrew, and Smith (1967) on the controversial school segregation-desegregation issue. Both authors had access to the same data, reports by study groups stating that the American educational system had failed in fourteen generations of schooling to provide an equal educational opportunity for the black student both quantitatively and qualitatively. Alsop (1967a) concluded that de facto segregation could not be ended in the near future. He stated that plans for large-scale bussing of children to integrate schools would be inadequate to meet the problem, should be ended, and the resources put into local improvement programs. Alsop (1967a) defined the situation by concluding that quality education must be brought into the ghetto providing the black community with the resources to remove themselves from a bad situation.

Using the same set of data, Schwartz, Pettigrew, and Smith disagreed with Alsop (1967a). They concluded that de facto segregation and its consequent educational inequality could be eliminated by massive bussing and mandatory integration of the nation's schools. They believed that to attempt what Alsop (1967a) recommended, keeping the schools the way they are and improving them qualitatively, would be a disasterous course that would contribute to the two separate racial societies forming in America today.

How does the reader make sense of these diverse and well-argued definitions of the situation? Which argument is based on a false definition of the situation: Alsop's or Schwartz, Pettigrew, and Smith's, or both? How do we decide which programs, if implemented on a large scale, would lead to beneficial results and which ones would lead to a disasterous self-fulfilling prophecy? How do we decide what beneficial means? Questions such as these are not easy to answer. They demand much study and thought, and although even then it may not be possible to decide which is which, they are the material from which good sociology is made.

C. CONCEPT CLARIFICATION PROJECTS

In Section C you have an opportunity to illustrate your understanding of the previously discussed concepts. In answering the following questions, combine your personal insights and experiences with the new information gained from your readings here and in *Social Change in Urban America.*

Questions Requiring Short Paragraph Answers

1. a. Name three different types of social systems other than those already mentioned. State why they are systems.
    b. Take a social system containing at least five different people and state briefly the details of their interrelationship and interdependency.
    c. Why is the institution of education known as a social system?

2. a. List the different social systems that are part of the school system. Diagram their hierarchical relationship to one another. Show which is higher or more powerful in terms of control of other systems.
    b. For some time now you have been in school. What are the major intellectual, social, and manual skills you have learned?
    c. Why have you been taught these skills and not others? For what position in society do they prepare you? How do they differ from the skills taught to your friends?
    d. Name another agent of formal socialization. Tell how it is similar to and different from the school system in its selection of the information it conveys.

3. a. Why is the school classroom the cornerstone of the school system? Is it more important in the long run than, for example, the school committee? Could there be a school without classes?
    b. What are the values you have learned during your education? How were they transmitted to you?
    c. Are the basic values learned in school different from those of other countries? Give examples.
    d. Focus on an ethnic group you know. List its unique ethnic values and discuss how they are transmitted and operate within a school classroom.

4. a. Take one example of a definition of the situation from your family life, one from your social life, and one from your school life. Explain the situations and consequences that you feel resulted.
    b. Give three definitions of the situation that became self-fulfilling prophecies, with at least one pertaining to you personally.
    c. Give two examples from your educational experience of self-fulfilling prophecies and their consequences. Could these have been avoided? How?

Summary Questions

The following topics require more thought and more detailed answers. Think carefully about the multiple interpretations possible for each topic and then prepare an answer that is as encompassing as possible. Use your own observations, interpretations, and readings in preparing your responses.

1. Is a city a social system?

2. How has urbanism influenced the school system of your community?

3. Explain the different teaching of cultural and ethnic values in a suburban and a ghetto classroom. If you see differences, why do they exist? If you perceive no differences, explain why this might be so.

D. EXAMPLES OF EDUCATION FIELD PROJECTS

1. A Detailed Example of an Education Field Project

The Problem   Three people decided to compare the reference groups of pupils in an inner city and a suburban school, hoping to show the influence of race and social class on reference group selection. The concept reference group is the set of persons whom an individual regards as socially significant to himself. They wanted to find out how much of the pupils' attitudes and behavior were the results of reference-group influence. They decided to measure high school seniors' selection and use of reference groups assuming that the influence of reference groups would be realted to their future plans.

The Hypothesis   The independent variable was the strength of the reference group's influence, and the dependent variable, the effect of the reference group on pupils' future plans. They hypothesized that if reference groups have an influence on high school seniors, reference groups will influence high schools' future plans. The amount of influence is directly related to the strength of the reference group—the stronger the influence of the reference group on the pupils' lives, the stronger is this influence on their choice of future plans.

Data Collection   By using a standard procedure allowing little variation in responses, they decided they would get the best information comparing inner-city and suburban high school seniors. They would give comparable sets of data-allowing analysis by constructing a questionnaire asking the same questions of pupils in both groups. Having decided on a technique, they then designed a questionnaire to measure the variables they wanted to test. This required developing questions measuring the kind and strength of the pupils' reference groups (the independent variable) and the effect of reference groups on the pupils' future plans (the dependent variable). Discussing and evaluating potential questions was difficult and time-consuming.

After completing a initial selection of questions they pre-tested them on a few respondents similar to those in the project population. The pre-test reduced the questionnaire's size from 20 to 10 items. These included items to measure the kind of reference group important to the pupil, the strength of the reference group, the future plans of the pupils, and the effect of the reference group on future plans. Following is the questionnaire they used.

Questions to Measure the Strength and Effort of Reference Groups on High School Seniors' Plans

Part One

1. Which of the following groups are you most a member of? (check one)
    a. hippies
    b. students
    c. kids on the corner
    d. parents and family
    e. other adults (friends, teachers, etc.)
    f. another group not mentioned (write in its name)
    g. no group

    [This question measured the kind of reference group the pupil felt was most important to him.]

2. How many of your good friends are in the group you mentioned? (check one)
    a. all or most of them
    b. some of them
    c. a few or none of them

    [This question, and the next three (3-5), measure the independent variable, the strength of the reference group. If the pupil checked the first alternative, the influence of the group was strong and his answer was given a 3. If the pupil checked the second alternative, the influence of the reference group was moderate and his answer was given a 2. If the pupil checked the third alternative, the influence of the reference group was weak and his answer was given a 1. This scoring procedure is followed throughout the questionnaire, as all questions have three alternatives.]

3. How much of your free time do you spend with this group? (check one)
    a. all or most of it
    b. some of it
    c. little or none of it

4. Do you enjoy doing the things your group does? (check one)
    a. all or most of the time
    b. some of the time
    c. little or none of the time

5. How close are you to other members of your group in what you believe? (check one)
    a. very close
    b. somewhat close
    c. not very close

Part Two

6. What do you plan to do after you graduate? (check one)
   a. go to college
   b. go to vocational school
   c. work
   d. go into the military
   e. do not know
   f. other (specify)

7. Who helped you come to this decision? (check as many as you need)
   a. hippies
   b. students
   c. kids on the corner
   d. parents and family
   e. other adults (friends, teachers, etc.)
   f. another group not mentioned (write in its name)
   g. no group

[This question and the next three (8-10), measure the dependent variable, the effect of the reference group. The scoring of this question differed from that of the next three, which follow the procedure outlined under question 2. If the student checked 1 or 2 groups and one of the groups was the same as the reference group, it indicates that the effect of the reference group was strong and he was given a 3. If he checked 3 or 4 groups and one was the same as his reference group, it indicates that the effect of the reference group was moderate and he was given a 2. If he checked 5 or more groups or 1 to 4 groups without the reference group, it indicates that the effect of the reference group was weak and he was given a 1.]

8. How many people in your group will be doing the same thing as you next year? (check one)
   a. all or most of them
   b. some of them
   c. a few or none of them

9. How will your decision for the future be accepted by your group? (check one)
   a. very easily
   b. somewhat easily
   c. not very easily

10. In five years, how alike do you think you and the others in your group will be? (check one)
    a. very much alike
    b. somewhat alike
    c. little alike

The researchers administered the questionnaire to high school seniors. To obtain the suburban high school pupils, they administered the questionnaire at a suburban high school during lunch hour. They tried to be random, going from lunch table to lunch table and testing one person from each table that included seniors.

To obtain the inner-city high school pupils they followed the same procedure. They were admitted to the lunch hour by school officials and spoke with seven seniors during this time. Because the lunch hour was arranged by sections, they interviewed pupils studying vocational training because this group happened to have lunch at this time. Realizing that this group might distort their study, they tried to get permission to stay for later lunch periods. This was not possible, and since they did not have time to return to the school, they had to use these responses.

Analysis   They first sorted all responses according to the strength of the reference group, using their scoring method. To measure reference group strength, the total score for questions 2-5 was calculated. If the score for these items was between 9 and 12, reference-group strength was strong. If the score was 5 to 8, reference-group strength was moderate. If the score was 1 to 4, reference-group strength was weak. The same procedure measured the reference group's effect. If the score for questions 7-10 was between 9 and 12, the reference group's effect was strong. If the score was between 5 and 8, the ference group's effect was moderate. If the score was between 1 and 4, the reference group's effect was weak.

They presented their results in the following tables.

TABLE 1. Type of Reference Group Important and Future Plans by Type of Pupil[a]

Type of Reference Group	Type of Pupil	
	Inner City High School	*Suburban High School*
kids on the corner	6	0
students	1	8
Total	7	8
Future Plans		
work	5	0
military service	1	0
college	1	8
Total	7	8

[a]Questions 1 and 6.

Table 1 compares the pupils in the two high schools. The inner-city and suburban pupils identify with different groups. The inner-city seniors name "kids on the corner" as the primary reference group, and suburban seniors name their fellow "students". This indicates the different social systems within which the two groups of pupils exist. The two groups' future plans closely follow the social patterns of the two groups; the inner-city seniors choosing work as their most immediate future, and the suburban seniors choosing college.

TABLE 2. Comparison of the Strength and Effect of Reference Groups on Future Plans of High School Seniors in Inner City and Suburban High Schools[a]

| | | Type of Pupil | |
| | | Inner City High School | Suburban High School |
Strength of Reference Group		Effect of Reference Group	Effect of Reference Group
strong	strong	3	5
	moderate	1	0
	weak	1	1
moderate	strong	0	1
	moderate	1	1
	weak	0	0
weak	strong	0	0
	moderate	0	0
	weak	1	0
Total		7	8

[a]Questions 2-5 and 7-10.

Table 2 gives the results for all pupils and compares the results of the inner-city group with the suburban group. Reference group effect is direct no matter whether the effect was strong, moderate, or weak. This influence is less direct among the inner-city seniors, possibly because the group of inner-city seniors chosen were vocationally trained. Other inner-city seniors may have a different group as their reference. The inner-city seniors may have more freedom in choosing future plans because of the diverse nature of their reference group—"kids on the corner"—or the difference may lie in the small size of the sample.

Table 3 combines inner-city and suburban groups to show the relationship between the independent and dependent variables. This table indicates the strong effect of reference groups on high school seniors' future plans. In Table 3, 73 percent of the strong reference group category showed a strong effect.

Final conclusions were weakened by the researchers' realization that their questionnaire was not clear. When they administered it to the two groups, as careful as they had been, the inner-city seniors had more difficulty understanding the questions. The suburban pupils were used to taking tests and questionnaires, and the inner-city pupils were not. The questionnaire had to be interpreted to the inner-city pupils, and the researchers were uncertain about the effect of this differential treatment. These difficulties are important extraneous variables. From their project the researchers learned much about themselves and about sociological research, and from a personal standpoint, the project was successful.

TABLE 3. Strength and Effect of Reference Groups on the Future Plans
of High School Seniors

Strength of Reference Groups	Effect of Reference Group	
strong	strong	8
	moderate	1
	weak	2
moderate	strong	1
	moderate	2
	weak	0
weak	strong	0
	moderate	0
	weak	1
Total		15

2. Other Examples of Education Field Projects

a. Styles of teaching

The Problem   The failure of education in inner-city areas is sometimes attrib-
uted to the way in which the teacher views his role. Three people were interested
in comparing teaching styles, of which they believed there are two major types:
traditional and progressive.

The Hypothesis   Their hypothesis was that a progressive teaching technique
would produce greater academic success in all pupils than would a traditional
technique.

Data Collection   The hypothesis was tested in two stages. In the first stage
the researchers observed teachers teaching in two elementary school classrooms
and noted the methods they used and their effects. Each person involved in the
project visited the two classrooms separately, on different days, to make observations without conferring with one another. This separation prevented one set of
observations from biassing others. In the second stage each person interviewed
the two teachers, using a prepared set of questions. The results of the two stages
were tabulated, compared with one another, and, with the pupils' academic
records, used to measure academic success.

Analysis   There were many confounding variables they could not cope with
in this analysis. One of the teachers had been teaching ten years and the other
one year. One of the teachers was black and teaching in a predominantly black
school, and the other was white and teaching in a predominantly black school.
The researchers were not able to formally accept or reject the hypothesis. After
taking their difficulties into account, they thought the differences they expected
were, if anything, opposite to the predicted direction. The pupils of the progressive teacher did not do as well academically as those of the traditional teacher.

b. The tutoring problem

The Problem   Four persons were interested in the academic success or failure of children in an inner-city tutoring program. They were interested in comparing the pupils' perception of the tutoring situation with the school department's view of the program.

The Hypothesis   Prior study led the researchers to think that pupils who needed tutoring had negative images of themselves as learners and would have difficulty overcoming this self-fulfilling prophecy. They hypothesized that if the pupils in the tutoring program had negative self-images, they would show little progress in their tutored subjects.

Data Collection   The information was collected in two ways, by unstructured interviews with school officials in charge of the tutoring program, and by evaluation of the pupils' self-images.

Analysis   The data were mixed but the researchers detected a pattern in their results. They worked with six pupils throughout the project, and four had negative images of themselves as learners. These four did not improve in their regular classes as a result of the tutoring. The two pupils with positive self-images showed varying levels of scholastic improvement after tutoring. The researchers concluded that tutoring makes little difference to pupils with negative self-images. This conclusion was interesting because interviews with school officials indicated that they believed tutoring has a positive effect for all pupils.

c. Pupils' attitudes toward school

The Problem   Three persons had read about pupils in public schools disliking school and wanted to find out if this was true.

The Hypothesis   They compared three groups of public school pupils: inner city, inner-city advanced (pupils in an educational enrichment program), and suburban. They hypothesized that given the potential for career success in each group—the suburban highest, inner-city advanced middle, and inner city least—suburban pupils would like school most, inner-city advanced second, and inner city would like it least.

Data Collection   To test their hypothesis they constructed a questionnaire to be administered to the three groups of pupils.

Analysis   They found support for their hypothesis. The inner-city pupils had negative attitudes toward school, the inner-city advanced were less negative, and the suburban pupils were the least negative. Differences between inner-city advanced and suburban pupils were not as large as expected. The inner-city advanced pupils seemed to like school very much, just slightly less than the suburban school pupils. This was unexpected, and the researchers interpreted it as meaning that inner-city advanced pupils responded to school more positively because of their opportunity to take subjects they enjoyed, the noticeable interest taken in them by their teachers, and the excellent modern facilities of their school.

d. The teacher's definition of the situation

The Problem Much writing argues that inner-city schools are failures because the teachers tend to give up and perform routinely. Two people wished to find out what changes occurred in teachers' attitudes towards teaching as a result of a number of years in service.

The Hypothesis The literature reviewed led them to think that the longer a teacher was in service, the more his attitudes toward teaching would change from excitement to boredom.

Data Collection They designed a questionnaire for data collection to administer to thirty teachers, fifteen from each of two schools. They constructed measures of excitement and boredom. For comparison purposes they grouped teachers into five categories by length of service: 1-2 years, 3-4 years, 5-6 years, 6-10 years, and more than 10 years.

Analysis They had trouble with their questionnaire. In the pre-tests, they saw that they had incorrectly constructed measures of the variables boredom and excitement. They drafted the questionnaire again and pre-tested it. Although it appeared successful, the final results were so diverse that they were not able to make any conclusions about the hypothesis.

This project was confused because the respondents were very nonrepresentative. Some teachers refused to answer the questionnaire, and some items on the questionnaire were not understood even after two pre-tests. They decided to try the project again after having learned something about problem finding and problem solving.

e. Parents and change in educational programs

The Problem Two persons were intrigued about the interest and effect of pupils' parents on the educational programs in a suburban area.

The Hypothesis This project was exploratory, seeking to measure the impact of parents' interests on educational programs. They sought to discover how many of the educational programs parents felt were important would be put into effect during a five-year period.

Data Collection To collect the necessary information for a decision, they used many techniques. To find out what programs parents wanted, they studied the minutes of the local PTA meetings for a five-year period. They content analyzed them for programs suggested or supported by parents. To get some understanding of the relationship of parents to school administration, they attended ten PTA meetings, going twice to five schools in the community. To find out the outcome of various programs, they interviewed six community officials and ten PTA-attending parents.

Analysis Parents had a great influence in determining school programs. Over a five-year period, fifteen programs had either been introduced or supported by parents. Of these fifteen, six pertained to basic changes in the instructional program, four were about allocation of funds, and five were about other areas such as recruitment of teachers. In the two latter categories, all the programs suggested were quickly implemented. In the basic change category, only three of the six programs were implemented and two of these took a long time to be done, three to five years to reach full strength. Despite resistance to basic changes in school policies, twelve of the fifteen programs introduced or supported by parents were implemented in this school system—evidence for the effect of parents on educational programs.

3. Suggestions for Education Field Projects

The political function of the school system is a major emphasis in the study of schools because schools operate at the center of many cross-pressures. The degree of politicization is indicated by the number and variety of voices influencing education. The schools are prone to be a focal point in issues of political control because all members of the society see education as crucial to their self-interest. Schools serve the interests of a factory city in that they turn out people capable and willing to do factory work. In a manufacturing city there will be pressure from the business community to have more vocational courses. In a suburban community where many residents are college graduates, there are pressures on the schools to emphasize college-oriented programs.

Another way of viewing education is to analyze and compare the values that influence the educational system—which are explicit, which are implicit? Understanding the role of values may make many of the concrete operations of the schools more comprehensible.

The teacher's lifestyle is an important aspect of education. In the daily operation of a school, the teacher's background of interests, beliefs, and values have an important influence. His effect on his pupils may last for years or even a lifetime without their being aware of it.

Sample Topics

1. One could develop a questionnaire to determine how certain categories of respondents see the schools; how they define the school situation. Do they see the schools in educational terms, in political terms, or as a combination of the two? For comparison the questionnaire could be administered to a group of business leaders in the community, a group of political leaders, and a group of educators.

2. Analysis of fund allocation in the school budget might reveal the community's attitudes. Public votes by elected representatives on bond issues and the school budget indicate the community's feelings about the conduct of the schools. One could try to determine motivations that led electorates to pass or reject previous bond issues or budgets.

3. Political ambitions may dictate the use of education to change the social order. Similarly political is the ambition of other elements in the community to maintain the schools according to the status quo. A stability index of a community might be tested by gaining reactions to disputed issues such as sex education, international studies, and ethnic studies.

4. It is obvious that teachers are becoming a political force. In New York City, the teachers' union has become actively involved in politics. Disputes over wages and benefits have resulted in strikes throughout the country. What evidence is there that such organization is also forming in your community? What evidence is there of your local teachers' organizations becoming political? How will such operations affect the future of the educational system in your area? Will it result in different values being taught in the schools?

5. One might interview parents of inner-city children about to enter first grade, those with children midway through elementary school, and those with children in secondary school, simulating a developmental sequence, to assess goals and values parents have for their children and how they change during a child's school career. These findings could be contrasted with parallel findings for middle-class parents and for differing racial and ethnic groups. Many combinations are possible, sorted by class, race, ethnicity, and stage of the child's development. This type of research shows whether race or social class influences expectations and implicit educational values of different groups.

6. It might be hypothesized that black parents have higher expectations for their children than do other ethnic groups. To what degree do black parents reject training and vocational education in favor of college preparatory objectives as compared with other similarly situated ethnic groups? One way to test this would be to take a range of school subjects and ask parents to rank the subjects in order of importance. This tests the hypothesis that many black parents' expectations about what schools should offer are high because of the difficulty of their school experiences. It would also be informative to compare the results of the parents' ranking with those of the children themselves or with the children's teachers. Children should make the most progress when all are in agreement.

7. One could test the assumption that cultural conflict exists in the school between the lower class child and the middle class teacher, comparing the objectives and values of the inner-city teachers for their students and the students' own objectives and values. The results could be compared by social class categories to determine if discrepancies exist.

8. Finding out who are considered the most successful teachers in an inner-city school would be indirect evidence of the school's hierarchy of educational values as well as uncovering self-fulfilling prophecies. One could hypothesize that the most successful teachers would be those teaching the high I.Q. college preparatory courses while teachers considered least successful would be teaching the lower I.Q. students.

9. It is frequently said that inner-city children are likely to have had significant ambitions at an early age, but repeated school failure has resulted in scaled-down aspirations. This proposition might be tested longitudinally in several groups of pupils by measuring school achievement of inner-city children. This project provides data about the immediate situation and the development of the process. As a control group, another group of pupils might provide comparable data on the school achievement of middle class children.

10. Popular opinion holds that educators are very conventional. This belief is manifested in a tendency to be punitive for misbehavior, to be strict about dress codes, and to reward quiet and conformist classroom behavior. Popular opinion also holds that educators have conventional attitudes regarding societal norms about marriage, sex, religion, and the values of achievement and economic wealth. One could test if this is

true by comparing educators with another occupational group on their attitudes about these topics.

E. SUPPLEMENTARY BIBLIOGRAPHY

Alsop, Joseph.
    1967a   "No more nonsense about ghetto education." *New Republic* (July 22):18-23.
    1967b   "Ghetto Education." *New Republic* (November 18):18-23.
Altshuler, Alan.
    1970   *Community Control: The Black Demand for Participation in Large American Cities.* New York: Pegasus.
Backer, Howard.
    1952a   "The career of the Chicago public school teacher." *American Journal of Sociology* 57 (March):470-477.
    1952b   "Social class variations in teacher-pupil relationships." *Journal of Educational Sociology* 25 (April):451-465.
Bernstein, Abraham.
    1967   *The Education of Urban Populations.* New York: Random House.
Bidwell, Charles.
    1965   "The school as a formal organization," pp. 972-1022 in James G. March (ed.), *Handbook of Organizations.* Skokie, Ill.: Rand McNally.
Birnbaum, Max.
    1964   "Whose values should be taught?" *Saturday Review* 47 (June 20):60-62.
Campbell, Ronald, et al.
    1965   *The Organization and Control of American Schools.* Columbus, Ohio: Merrill.
Cervantes, Lucius F.
    1965   *The Drop-Out: Causes and Cures.* Ann Arbor: University of Michigan Press.
Coleman, James B.
    1966   *Equality of Educational Opportunity.* Washington, D.C.: United States Office of Education.
Coles, Robert.
    1967   *Children of Crisis: A Study of Courage and Fear.* Boston: Little, Brown.
Dentler, R. A., et al.
    1967   *The Urban R's.* New York: Praeger.
Dentler, R. A., and Mary Ellin Warshauer.
    1965   *Big City Drop-Outs and Illiterates.* New York: Praeger.
Duncan, B.
    1967   "Education and social background." *American Journal of Sociology* 72 (January):363-372.
Dynes, W.
    1967   "Education and tolerance; analysis of intervening factors." *Social Forces* 46 (September):22-34.
Fantini, Mario, Marilyn Gittell, and Richard Magat.
    1970   *Community Control and the Urban School.* New York: Praeger.
Fuchs, Estelle.
    1968   "How teachers learn to help children fail." *Trans*-action 5 (September):45-49.
Gage, N.
    1963   *Handbook of Research on Teaching.* Skokie, Ill.: Rand McNally.
Gittell, Marilyn.
    1967   *Participants and Participation.* New York: Praeger.
    1968   *Six Urban School Districts.* New York: Praeger.

Goldstein, Bernard, et al.
    1967   *Low Income Youth in Urban Areas: Critical Review.* New York: Holt, Rinehart & Winston.

Gross, Neal.
    1959   "The sociology of education," pp. 128-152 in Robert Merton (ed.), *Sociology Today.* New York: Basic Books.

Gross, Neal, et al.
    1958   *Explorations in Role Analysis: The School Superintendent.* New York: Wiley.

Gross, Ronald, and Beatrice Gross (eds.).
    1970   *Radical School Reform.* New York: Simon & Schuster.

Halsey, H. H., Jean Floud, and C. A. Anderson (eds.).
    1960   *Education, Economy, and Society.* New York: Free Press.

Hansen, Donald, and Joel Gerstl.
    1967   *On Education: Sociological Perspectives.* New York: Wiley.

Haskins, Jim.
    1970   *Diary of a Harlem Schoolteacher.* New York: Grove.

Hillson, M.
    1967   "Reorganization of the school." *Phylon* 28 (Fall):230-245.

Holt, John.
    1970a   *How Children Fail.* New York: Dell.
    1970b   *How Children Learn.* New York: Dell.
    1970c   *The Underachieving School.* New York: Dell.

Hurd, G. E., and T. J. Johnson.
    1967   "Education and development." *Sociological Review* 15 (March):59-71.

Iannacone, Lawrence.
    1967   *Politics in Education.* New York: Center for Applied Research in Education.

Jencks, Christopher.
    1968   "Private schools for black children." *New York Times Magazine* (November 3): 304.

Jensen, Arthur R.
    1969   "How much can we boost I.Q. and scholastic achievement?" *Harvard Educational Review* 39 (Winter):1-123.

Keller, Suzanne.
    1963   "The social world of the urban slum child." *American Journal of Orthopsychiatry* 33:824-831.

Kerber, August, and Barbara Bommarito (eds.).
    1965   *The Schools and the Urban Crisis.* New York: Holt, Rinehart & Winston.

Kohl, Herbert.
    1968   *36 Children.* New York: New American Library.

Kozol, Jonathan.
    1967   *Death at an Early Age.* New York: Beacon.

Leonard, George.
    1968   *Education and Ecstasy.* New York: Delacorte.

Levin, Henry M.
    1970   *Community Control of Schools.* Washington, D.C.: The Brookings Institution.

Mayer, Martin.
    1969   *The Teachers' Strike.* New York: Harper & Row.

Miller, Harry L., and Marjorie Smiley.
    1967   *Education in the Metropolis.* New York: Free Press.

Moles, Oliver C.
    1965   "Training children in low income families for school." *Welfare in Review* 3 (June):1-11.

Moore, Alexander.
 1967   *Realities of the Urban Classroom: Observations in Elementary Schools.* Garden
         City, N.Y.: Doubleday.
Morrison, R.
 1967   "Education for environmental concerns." *Daedalus* 12 (Fall):10-33.
Parsons, Talcott.
 1959   "The school class as a social system: some of its functions in American society."
         Harvard Educational Review 29 (Fall):297-318.
Postman, Neil, and Charles Weingartner.
 1969   *Teaching as a Subversive Activity.* New York: Delacorte.
Reiss, Albert J. (ed.).
 1966   *Schools in a Changing Society.* New York: Free Press.
Resnik, Henry S.
 1970   *Turning on the System: War in the Philadelphia Public Schools.* New York:
         Pantheon.
Ribich, Thomas I.
 1968   *Education and Poverty.* Washington, D.C.: The Brookings Institution.
Riesman, David.
 1958   *Constraint and Variety in American Education.* Garden City, N.Y.: Doubleday.
Roberts, Joan (ed.).
 1967   *School Children in the Urban Slums.* New York: Free Press.
Rogers, David.
 1968   "New York City schools: a sick bureaucracy." *Saturday Review* (July 20):47.
Rosenthal, Alan.
 1969   *Pedagogues and Power: Teacher Groups in School Politics.* Syracuse: Syracuse
         University Press.
Schrag, Peter.
 1965   *Voices in the Classroom.* Boston: Beacon.
 1967   *Village School Downtown.* Boston: Beacon.
Schreiber, Daniel (ed.).
 1964   *The School Drop-Out.* Washington, D.C.: National Education Association.
Schueler, H.
 1965   "Education in the modern urban setting." *Law and Contemporary Problems* 30
         (Winter):162-175.
Schwartz, Robert, Thomas Pettigrew, and Marshall Smith.
 1967   "Fake panaceas for ghetto education." *New Republic* (September 23):16-19.
Silberman, Charles.
 1970   *Crisis in the Classroom.* New York: Random House.
Smith, Louis M., and William Geffrey.
 1968   *The Complexities of an Urban Classroom: An Analysis toward a General Theory
         of Teaching.* New York: Holt, Rinehart & Winston.
Snyder, E. E.
 1968   "Sociology of education." *Sociology and Social Research* 52 (January):237-242.
Stinchecombe, Arthur L.
 1964   *Rebellion in a High School.* Chicago: Quadrangle.
Strow, Robert (ed.).
 1966   *The Inner City Classroom: Teacher Behaviors.* Columbus, Ohio: Merrill.
Toby, Jackson.
 1957   "Orientation to education as a factor in school maladjustment of lower-class
         children." *Social Forces* 35 (March):259-266.
Waller, Willard.
 1932   *The Sociology of Teaching.* New York: Wiley.

Wasserman, Miriam.
    1970   *The School Fix, New York City, U.S.A.* New York: Outerbridge & Dienstfrey.
Wise, Arthur E.
    1968   *Rich Schools, Poor Schools: The Promise of Equal Educational Opportunity.*
            Chicago: University of Chicago Press.
Wolf, Eleanor, and Leo Wolf.
    1962   "Sociological perspectives on the education of culturally deprived children."
            School Review 70 (Winter):73-87.

4

Police

A. INTRODUCTION

In Chapter 4 we present aspects of the police public service bureaucracy. Section B defines sociological concepts applicable to the police selected from *Social Change in Urban America*. The concept clarification projects in Section C provide an opportunity to use the new concepts in investigating the significance of the police in the community. Section D includes potential field projects about police drawn from actual studies. It has three subsections, the first one presenting a detailed example of a police field project applying the five research steps involved. This is a chronological account including successes and failures, obstacles and insights that actually took place. It emphasizes that field projects, as all sociological investigation, are social processes themselves; the route from initial idea formulation to outcome is not neat and predictable. The second subsection, Other Examples of Police Field Projects, presents brief accounts of five field projects to give an idea of the variety and sources of information available. The third subsection, Suggestions for Field Projects, includes possible focal points for study of the police. These listings are not complete but are suggestive of the range of possibilities. Section E contains a supplementary bibliography about the police, a source for additional information and ideas.

B. CONCEPTS

1. Social Control

A community is a fragile entity; its continued existence presumes the mutual acknowledgement of its members of the appropriate ways to act. Coherence, predictability, and order in social life are the outcomes of people behaving similarly in similar situations. Traffic stops at red lights and moves at green lights; people scheduled to begin work at nine o'clock arrive at work by about nine o'clock. Much of the order and predictability is a product of socialization, unceasing informal learning in which we all continuously participate. Through socialization we learn when and how to do various things and who are our most appropriate information sources. Socialization teaches accepted sets of responses to specific situations. By rewards and benefits, social control agents teach us the limits of accepted behavior; by reprimand and punishment, when these limits have been exceeded.

Social control is always mediated by an agent. Parents are the first social control agents encountered by the growing child. They teach behavior and attitudes which are acceptable and prevent ones which are not. Unacceptable responses are greeted by negative sanctions, a form of punishment administered by the social control agent. The visibility of punishment for exceeding the limits of acceptable behavior has two purposes. First, punishment is intended to be unpleasant for the person who commits the illegal behavior; its negative character and public nature diminish the possibility that the offender will want to perform that negatively rewarded behavior again. Secondly, punishing an offender aims to deter others who might have thought of performing the same act. Overt punishment has a deterrent effect on others by reinforcing the necessity of acceptable behavior.

For the child, the father is the primary agent of social control; for the community, it is the police force. In a community the main task of the police force is to maintain order through the use of social control. Elements of police work that heighten visibility are deliberate; wearing a uniform and riding in marked patrol cars remind us of the consequences of misbehavior.

A police force is important to community functioning because it is a primary agent of community social control. The police make decisions with immediate consequences for the character of social life. The policeman has significant jurisdiction; very often the application of a law depends on his definition of the situation and his discretion. In actuality he must define what falls into the category of legal and illegal.

The policeman is a powerful community worker with great authority. We can say that they are often father figures for their community; not, however, for all segments of the community, as the use of the epithet "pigs" has recently indicated. Policemen are vitally responsible for continued order and predictability in the community. As an agent of social control, the policeman supports a role that is conservative and stabilizing. Police activity is expected to reflect the dominant values and norms of the community whose laws it is enforcing.

2. Role and Role Conflict

As commonly used in sociology, a role is the behavior of a person who occupies a status in a community or organization. We speak of the status or position of policemen in a community when we describe his social characteristics—age, social class, daily schedules. If we look at what policemen do in the community, we examine the policemen's role, the behavioral dimension of his social position.

There are two principal ways to analyze role: ideal and actual role behavior. Ideal role is the complex of defined ways of behaving learned by neophytes during their initial training. The ideal role can never be performed in its totality. People learn the ideal role as a set of overall behavioral patterns they should try to emulate. Thus no person ever completely achieves his image of the ideal role. Variables of personality, situation, and variation in socialization prevent any two people from displaying role behavior in complete agreement with the ideal role. Nevertheless, in spite of these variables, two policemen behave more like each other than do two people in different roles.

The other conceptualization of role, actual role, is the individual's behavior in a particular status position. When we see a policeman walking his beat, we see actual role behavior. This is the personal manifestation of ideal role behavior learned through socialization.

The interactional nature of social life intensifies the distinction between actual and ideal roles. As a product of interaction, social life is formed through networks of reciprocal linkages which are social systems. Because every interaction involves different people playing different roles, no interaction is completely predictable. The interaction between a policeman arresting an elderly alcoholic may differ from the same policeman's apprehension of a speeding motorist. The policeman thinks and acts according to the interactional situation defined by the other person, his status, the physical situation, and the policeman's emotional outlook at that moment. The other person's expectations influence the policeman's actions by calling out and rewarding certain responses. The variability of the policeman's behavior explains somewhat the many images we hold of him—helper, scolder, arrester, overreactor, or advisor.

The discrepancy between idealized images and actual tasks of police work form the basis for the report by Cumming et al. (1965) on the role conflicts policemen experience. Policemen are trained for social control functions—arresting, warning, chasing, catching people who threaten the community's order. But much police work involves social support—helping elderly people, transporting the sick, counseling troubled youths, intervening in family quarrels. Police training in supportive or helping techniques is minimal compared with the amount of time given to training for the other activities.

In addition to a lack of training and resources for supportive actions, policemen have difficulty reconciling these different dimensions of their work role and allotting time to each facet of their work. Both tasks need to be done, and often police are criticized for failing in one area or the other, perhaps because they devoted too much time to performing only one. The demand that police perform supportive and control functions while in the police role is what is meant by role conflict. This situation results when one person must do two or more irreconcilable things due to conflicts in expectations, timing, location or type of work. The existence of excessive role conflict makes the role occupant uncomfortable and anxious about his role performance. He is personally unable to resolve the problems inherent in the vaguely defined role especially if his personality is rigid.

3. Police Secrecy

Policemen have a difficult position in the community. A police force is usually composed of community members who are guardians of the community's values and who must react severely to any threats to the community's order. Recruits trained to perform this caretaker function are in the process imbued with the zeal necessary to maintain community standards. Policemen have to be trained to act in an extraordinary way to protect aspects of community life that are taken for granted by its members. Their work is lonely work in that it isolates its practitioners from other members of the community. Because they are guardians of the legal code, some people react with aversion to friendships with them for fear of being discovered committing an illegal act.

Policemen have to be trained to a new personal perspective to be able to observe and react to violations of law and social disorder that others overlook. They must learn to react firmly toward lawbreakers. Most people's daily tasks require all their energy, so they do not notice a person who continually lurks in a particular area or the late model car with deliberately muddied license plates. Policemen develop the ability to notice these things.

The requirement that policemen must have heightened sensitivity to suspicious situations and strong reactions to law violations creates specifications for police training and an atmosphere within the police force differing from that of the community. Police training has a paramilitary tone, prescribing physical separation of the recruits, distinctive dress and naming systems, and a unique set of values. Secrecy allows separation of the police force's atmosphere from the community's, thus creating a subculture into which new members are initiated through training and first days on the job.

4. Adult Socialization and Police Personality

The separation of police from the community—the subculture elements of police organization—influence the policeman's personality. To transform police recruits into policemen, the training period is necessarily strong adult socialization. Brim and Wheeler (1966) classify adult socialization as change in visible behavior, attitudes, and opinions, distinguishing it from childhood socialization which establishes values and deeply rooted patterns. Adult socialization is redirection of overt dimensions of life in people with previously established value patterns.

In police training the recruit becomes familiar with new titles, formal and informal; adopts a new dress style, a uniform; and learns configurations with which to observe the rest of the world. Skolnick (1966) says the policeman's outlook is a product of his concern with authority and danger. The new policeman must learn that he is an authority figure and will be seen as one; he must incorporate this into his identity. He also learns that his world is filled with danger; at every moment he must be observant of possible danger to himself or others.

The public views policemen as separated from the community, as defenders of the community's standards. The aura surrounding the police also puts them at a distance from others. Police training must be dramatic in order to enable the new policeman to hold a role responded to in unusual ways. People perceive that policemen differ, and, according to the self-fulfilling prophecy, policemen learn to look at their community and act within it differently from laymen.

Not all of the public in any community views the police as defenders of their standards. In all cities, a large proportion of the inhabitants look upon the police almost as an alien occupying force. These people constitute the elements detached from the society's social and economic mainstream. While they want police protection and support, they tend to look on police behavior as intrusive, seeing the police as interfering with their lives. The police see them as potential enemies whose behavior is dangerous and unpredictable.

5. Police Career

The concept of career introduces the influence of time into police work. Just as being a police recruit differs from being a rookie cop, other stages of being a policeman differ. The concept of a police career conveys the influence that time spent in a role has on the way the role occupant thinks and acts.

The organization of a police force is unique because it rarely permits lateral entry. All members, regardless of how high a position they may hold, were once patrolmen. New members begin at the lowest level and advance into the higher ranks normally through a series of competitive exams.

Police work can be very discouraging. Everyone wants laws enforced but no one wants to be punished for infractions. Graft and favors are ways citizens and policemen establish informal procedures of preventing punishment for law breaking. With time policemen confront these informal negations of the harshness of law enforcement. Neiderhoffer (1967) reports that cynicism among policemen is associated with the policeman's length of time in service. The early idealism of the recruit and the rookie cop becomes tempered by the realities of trying to enforce the law, and the attitude shifts from idealism to a cynical realism.

6. Police Professionalism

Being a professional is very different from being a job holder. A professional—for example, a physician, a lawyer, or a minister—performs a skill the quality of which can only be judged by colleagues. Professional associations control the certification of other professionals. A professional is paid for performing his skill, a fee for service, and this he is willing to do whenever needed. A professional usually does not have a regular workday; his involvement with his work and the people he serves precludes such limitations. His work is an important component of his self-identity, and the merging of his work and self-identity influences his attitudes and values.

Within police work there is a strong dispute between those who see the police role as professional and those who see it as a job. Generally higher-ranking and better-educated policemen consider police work as professional work, which is keeping in line with their greater dedication and commitment. This distinction has much social significance; it creates a chasm within the police organization. The officers in command, being better-educated and with more responsibility, differ from the patrolmen in their idea of the police role. Intraorganizational stress and communication problems appear.

Walsh (1969) studied the consequences of holding professional and job orientations towards police work. Policemen who viewed themselves as professionals have more concern for the social and psychological dynamics of the problems they handle. Policemen who see themselves as job holders have stereotyped responses to social problems and favor rigid, repressive police response to social problems. The question of professionalism does have and will continue to have great repercussions for police work, specifically for the interpretation of the police role, police attitudes, and career goals. The multiple demands placed on the police may dictate restructured police forces. During this reevaluation the professionalism issue will have an important part in determining the outcome.

The President's Commission on Law Enforcement and the Administration of Justice (1967) has made the recommendation that the role of policemen be separated into three roles, distinguishing the social control, social support, and administrative components. The issue of occupational self-identity will be important for policemen in coming years.

C. CONCEPT CLARIFICATION PROJECTS

We have now discussed concepts basic to a mastery of the selections on police included in *Social Change in Urban America*. We include a set of concept clarification projects to allow the reader to demonstrate his ability to understand and apply these concepts.

Questions Requiring Short Paragraph Answers

1. a. Is social control necessary in society; in your community?
   b. Give some examples of social control.
   c. Give your opinion of the statement: The main purpose of punishment for criminals is to prevent others from doing the same thing.
   d. What would happen if there were no police force in your community?

2. a. What is a role?
   b. Give some examples of roles you play.
   c. What is the police role?
   d. Is the policeman ever off duty? What should he do if he sees a crime occurring on his day off?
   e. What does it mean to wear a uniform?

3. a. What is role conflict?
   b. Have you ever experienced role conflict in your own life? Give an example and include both the source of the conflict and its resolution.
   c. What are some ways of handling role conflict? How effective are they?
   d. What types of role conflict do policemen experience? How do they handle them?

4. a. What does police secrecy mean?

b. How does the absence of lateral entry into police work contribute to police secrecy?

c. What is the relationship between police secrecy and the existence of a police subculture?

d. Give some examples from your own life of your experiences within a subculture.

5. a. What is adult socialization? How extensive is it?

b. How does adult socialization differ from childhood socialization?

c. What are some of the changes that take place in a person starting a new job? Draw on your own experiences.

d. Why do the military, the police, the medical profession, and some other occupations have more rigid and formal introductory procedures than other types of employment such as retailing and manufacturing?

6. a. What is the effect of a man's work on his outlook on the world? Apply this specifically to the case of the police.

b. It is commonly said that with time police become cynical. What does this mean and why might it happen?

c. What is the sequence of personality change that new policemen undergo?

7. a. How does a police career differ from a career in business?

b. Is the markedly distinct nature of a police career necessary? If so, why?

8. a. What does being a professional mean? How does it differ from holding a job?

b. Do you think that policemen are professionals or can become professionals? How?

c. Would a sharper segregation of the professional and nonprofessional aspects of police work be an improvement? Or would it make police work increasingly paramilitary?

Summary Questions

The following topics require more thought and more detailed answers. Think carefully about the multiple interpretations possible for each topic and prepare an answer that is as encompassing as possible. Use your own observations, interpretations, and conclusions in preparing your responses.

1. In periods of stress, police paranoia increases. Policemen find themselves blamed and criticized for almost any action they take or fail to take. This raises the question of what do we expect of police, and is it unrealistic?

2. Human problems are often culture-bound. Policemen are accused of aggravating situations because they lack understanding of idiosyncratic problems. Should local control and recruitment of police be introduced? What would be the positive and negative consequences of this action?

3. Policemen often provide residual support services which other agencies overlook or deliberately avoid. Why is this so, and what alternatives are there?

4. Many policemen want to become more professional with all that it implies for education and specialization. What sorts of problems will arise for the community if all policemen are professionals?

5. Is the policeman a victim of our own psychological projections? Do we view him as a type of father figure and therefore expect the impossible from him?

6. Assuming that social control is integral to community cohesion, what alternatives can you devise to our current organization of police work?

D. EXAMPLES OF POLICE FIELD PROJECTS

1. A Detailed Example of a Police Field Project

The Problem Three people worked on this project. They wanted to evaluate community satisfaction with and the subjective impact of the police service. The backgrounds and career plans of the researchers influenced the project focus. One planned a career in law and public service, another was interested in community work and in joining VISTA, and the third had previously worked on programs to help minorities. The focus on the community's perception, evaluation, and recommendations for police work was related to their shared interest in the dynamics of community operation.

They mutually agreed that they wanted to measure community evaluation of police service. Theirs was an effort to substantiate the often-heard claim that people are dissatisfied with the police; that police do not perform all necessary functions. If this dissatisfaction exists, it should be more present in the black community which has experienced inadequate services and attention.

While there was unanimity on the main objective, community evaluation of police service, the researchers found it difficult to become specific about what they wanted to measure. This problem grew larger as they moved toward data collection. Uncertainty created some of the problems in the operation stage. Initially they translated community evaluation of police service into measuring whether residents of the black community felt they had adequate police protection.

Their intellectual ambition was to relate objective and subjective realities. The question arose: What is the correspondence between subjective perceptions and objective realities? More crime occurred in the black community than in other areas of the city, and the residents were the victims of this crime. Complaints about police inadequacies and inappropriate behaviors were frequent issues. There are the facts about police activities, crime, and the black community but they do not imply that the community residents are unhappy about their police protection. The project aimed to determine the residents' subjective evaluations of police effectiveness.

To gather information, they had to get opinions from a cross-section of the community. It is almost impossible to get complete and accurate listings of the residents in poor areas from which to sample; telephone books list people able to afford phones, and voting lists name people who have not moved recently. Time and limited manpower were also considerations. Therefore fairly unconventional techniques were necessary to obtain the desired information.

The Hypothesis This project was exploratory and did not hypothesize about the issue. Instead a careful problem statement was constructed. The problem studied was that residents of the black community think they do not have enough police protection. This problem statement subsumes the several dimensions of police work evaluated; quantity and quality of police service, community interpretation of the police role, and the way the community views itself in relation to the police.

Data Collection   Questions of administration became paramount—what sources could be used effectively to obtain the necessary information. These considerations became so important that they overshadowed the need to make their problem statement more concrete. One of the researchers was interested in radio broadcasting and hosted a discussion program beamed to the black community over the university radio station. They excitedly decided to air their questions as the program topic and record the telephone calls received. They viewed the radio discussion program as a format allowing additional probes to the telephone caller by the radio host. The question would be aired and open-ended responses would be received and recorded for subsequent analysis.

With administration questions answered, they drafted appropriate statements, which was very difficult. The statement had to be short to hold attention; clear, direct, and provocative to motivate people to telephone in their reactions. They devised a statement based on a quotation from a prominent person, which lent importance and credibility to the issue. The statement went:

In a statement made in January, Roy Wilkins, Executive Director of the NAACP, called for stiffer laws against mugging and for increased police protection for the people of Harlem. Do you as a resident of _____ feel this need exists in our community also? Yes? No? Why?

The study did not have a formal pre-test. Instead the researchers administered several revisions of the statement based on unanticipated problems revealed by the telephone callers' responses. The initial format was biased and suggested an answer to the caller. The phrasing asked for a "yes" or "no" response, and to get additional information, the host had to ask more questions. The additional questions varied according to the situation, making it difficult to interpret and compare responses. There were technical problems in obtaining tape recordings of the radio program. The station could not be relied on, and the researchers were not always there.

After completing this phase they realized they did not have enough information, so they tried a supplementary technique, a telephone survey of the black community. Although they recognized the bias in this procedure, they decided to risk it to get more data. Telephone calls were made to households listed in the metropolitan directory which lists numbers by communities. The selection procedure required opening the telephone directory randomly and pointing to a name. Initial telephone calls showed that the radio question was too long, involved, and complicated for the respondent, and that the researchers had to develop and explain the statement instead of presenting an unbiased statement.

They then created a revision for the telephone survey, using a simpler introduction, as well. The difficulty had been the complexity if the statement and the respondents' inability to relate meaningfully to the author of the idea and the location. These references were discarded, and they ended with three questions which proceeded clearly and elicited responses. The telephone survey went as follows:

> Hello, my name is _____. We're doing a survey in connection with _____ University. I'd like to ask you a question or two if I may. Do you feel the need for increased police protection in your neighborhood? What changes would you like to see in the way in which the police serve your neighborhood? Do you feel the problems are with the police department as a whole or just with the individual policemen in your neighborhood?

Despite operational difficulties, the researchers obtained interesting results. They learned the need for conceptual precision and the influence of words and their arrangement in suggesting responses. From conversational exchanges with their respondents they determined that they had higher educational and economic levels than had been anticipated. The university radio station drew a selective audience despite its aim to broadcast to the entire black community. Telephone listings unavoidably provide more affluent respondents.

Analysis Because they asked open-ended questions to stimulate discussion, they had to content analyze the respondents' phrases and sentences, looking for recurrent themes. Applying this technique to an exploratory study yields impressionistic, descriptive results. Consideration of the outcomes of this project generates more precise hypotheses with which to initiate rigorous analysis. From the responses, the researchers reported a universal interest in the need for increased police protection. One-third were dissatisfied with the policing of their neighborhoods and felt that the police were negligent and overlooked many things. This was a comment on police function rather than an attack on policemen personally. One-fourth of the respondents resented the question's being limited to the black community and believed that crime was widespread. Some respondents mentioned a recent change with the increased danger in the community and expressed nostalgia for the days "when it was safe to go out walking." Older women mentioned fear of getting hit and having their pocketbooks snatched.

The researchers were dissatisfied with the responses received from the radio program. The radio statement was too slanted and suggested a certain response. The question was not suited to their purposes, and they had to base much of their analysis on the telephone supplement.

The respondents' age range, estimated from conversation, influenced their evaluation of policy. Older people were conservative, supported the police strongly, and desired more police and stiffer treatment of criminals. Younger respondents viewed the police as intruders; they were conscious of the racial influences on treatment by policemen of people in the black community. Regardless of age, most respondents were aware of the racial dimension of police work. Some suggested more black policemen; others mentioned the need for more respect among the police for the community residents. Racial consciousness was widespread.

The researchers learned much from this field project. Their difficulties in operationalizing the problem showed the need for conceptual precision. The problems and inadequacies that appeared in the data collection instrument demonstrated the variable significance of words and phrases and the need for great care to create effective research measures.

From the outcomes they became aware of the need for improved personal contacts between police and community residents. The community judges police by their visible manifestations and does not go beyond these appearances. Members of racial minorities are aware of and resent discriminatory, condescending treatment. The black community suffers more from crime and would like more efficient, stringent, and equitable law enforcement.

2. Other Examples of Police Field Projects

a. Children's attitudes toward policemen

The Problem   Three people were interested in what lower class children thought of policemen and if age influenced their opinions. Reading suggested that children's attitudes towards policemen become increasingly negative with age.

The Hypothesis   The researchers hypothesized that as children grow older they have a more negative attitude toward policemen.

Data Collection   They interviewed elementary, junior high, and high school boys using a cross-sectional design to simulate change over time. The age variation created difficulties for data collection, because verbal skills, knowledge, and development of opinions vary in this age range. Each person worked with one of the three age groups and created an appropriate interview schedule. For the youngest children they used a simple interview with concrete response categories. The interview schedule for the junior high school age group required interpretation of cartoons. The high school interview was open-ended and conversational. As the respondent's age increased they used less structured techniques. Obtaining respondents by walking onto playgrounds located near public housing projects, they interviewed after school and used casual conversational situations.

The researchers constructed their interview schedules together so that although items differed, they measured the same variable. The three schedules covered the children's attitudes to dimensions of police work: attitudes towards policemen, frequency of contact with policemen, parental and peer group attitudes toward policemen, and activities of policemen in their neighborhood.

Analysis   They found that with age children report increasingly negative attitudes towards policemen. The elementary school children had friendly and positive attitudes, reflecting their contacts with policemen in school and on television.

Negative attitudes began to appear with the junior high school age group, this being the period when children become attached to peer groups and reject parental guidelines. Policemen are community guardians, surrogate father figures, and the adolescents hear about and meet policemen in repressive and punitive situations. The process is intensified among high school students; by this time the lower-class child is likely to have had negative contacts with police.

The development of negative attitudes towards policemen is a correlate of the policeman's guardian role. As adolescents escape their home's influence and attempt new things independently, they are likely to confront policemen in an adversary relationship.

b. Professionalism among policemen

The Problem Two people wanted to determine whether professionalism permeated policemen's self-identity, to see whether Neiderhoffer's (1967:24) list of the dimensions of police professionalism applied to policemen's perception of their role.

The Hypothesis This project was exploratory, and the problem statement was that policemen would have mixed reactions to characteristics of professionalism. The researchers thought the variables rank and number of years in the role influence policemen's self-identity as a professional, the former directly and the latter inversely.

Data Collection Using the points listed by Neiderhoffer (1967:24), they constructed an open-ended interview schedule to guide conversation. They interviewed six policemen of differing ranks and lengths of service from differing communities.

Analysis The respondents agreed that policemen could use more education. Higher-ranked policemen recommended college degrees while patrolmen wanted more practical training to help with specific areas of police work.

The policemen felt thwarted by the judicial process; their administration of justice was threatened and downgraded by the courts. The fact that policemen must act in concert with the courts diminishes police autonomy and creates status anxiety.

The findings of project agreed with Neiderhoffer (1967:23) that the hierarchical structure of the police force, manifested by ranks and pay differentials, hinders professionalism. Full-fledged professionals work in a collegial fashion because they consider other professionals equal on the basis of skill and responsibility.

Within a police force the higher-ranking members have a more professional self-image. The lack of agreement about whether policemen are to perform enforcement, support roles, or both diminishes professionalism, because professionals have clearly defined roles accepted by themselves and the general public. Professionalism remains a distant goal for policemen. Many areas still block a clear definition of the policeman as a professional.

c. The community and police force's understanding of the police role

The Problem Two people were interested in the congruence between community members' and policemen's opinions about the police role. They hoped by asking community residents and local policemen the same questions to show areas of agreement and dispute about police work. This project hoped to reveal reasons for community discontent with police.

The Hypothesis   This project was exploratory and measured the similarity between community residents' and policemen's opinions of the police role as community supporter, crime preventer, and professional. They concluded with several hypotheses about police-community relationships and the police role.

Data Collection   The technique used was an interview with a fixed-choice questionnaire format. They designed two parallel interview schedules with eleven questions each, one for community residents and the other for policemen. They interviewed six policemen of several ranks and twenty-five community members.

Analysis   Higher and lower-ranking policemen differed about the most important goals of their occupation, lower-ranking officers emphasizing crime prevention and higher-ranking ones emphasizing professionalism. They felt that policemen expect more of themselves as policemen than did the community. The community residents and the policemen agreed that more education would help policemen better understand their role.

Despite much negative publicity, the community residents did not have negative reactions toward police. There was a lack of mutual respect between policemen and the community residents. The community does not expect police professionalism, but the community needs to be more aware of the policemen and their tasks.

d. Differences between urban and rural police

The Problem   While reading about the police, one person became intrigued with Neiderhoffer's (1967:30) argument that the style of operation of a police department reflects the complexity and social structure of the community it serves. He posed the question: Does the nature of the community influence the structure of the police force and the work it does?

The Hypothesis   The basic idea stems from Durkheim's distinction between mechanical solidarity, with its tendency toward repressive law, and organic solidarity, with its tendency toward institutive legal actions. On these grounds the researcher hypothesized that certain police would be more concerned with "humane" problems than their rural counterparts.

Data Collection   The researcher selected two communities, 200 miles apart, for comparison—one a large city, the state capital, with a heterogeneous population; and the other a small, isolated, socially homogeneous, mainly agricultural community. The researcher analyzed each community's police structure and composition, which paralleled the respective community's social characteristics. Informal interviews with several policemen were conducted focussing on their police work, problems encountered, and responses to the problems.

Analysis   In the city, policemen were removed from the citizens and unaware of a neighborhood's operation and problems, whereas in the small community, there was no anonymity and no difficulty obtaining information; policemen were in close touch with everything. The city policemen's feeling of isolation from the citizens and emphasis on the danger and violence they faced contrasts with the personal quality of police work in the small community. The city policeman feels he must see his work as serious, that he needs to be efficient and businesslike.

In both communities policemen felt there were poor relationships between themselves and the community; they lacked the confidence and understanding of the public. Police seem to be controversial everywhere.

The project was unable to give a definite answer to the hypothesis that urban police are more humane than rural police. The problems of police work are too complex to be readily categorized. The criticism police feel, as well as their lack of effective contact with the community, may preclude the possibility of effective humane police work.

e. Attitude change in police recruits and college students

The Problem   One person studied police reaction to a college course on minorities. There was a pilot program in which police recruits were enrolled in sociology courses in addition to the conventional police training. The course policemen enrolled in was similar to a course given to undergraduates. The researcher compared the reactions to and evaluation of the course by the police recruits and the college students to measure the course's impact.

The Hypothesis   This project was exploratory and aimed to study whether police recruits welcome and learn from academic courses on social problems.

Data Collection   The project compared police and undergraduate responses to a course evaluation administered at the end of the course on minorities. The eight-item questionnaire asked respondents to evaluate both the adequacy of the course and the amount of learning gained. Ideally there should have been a questionnaire administered before the course began to measure the change in opinions, but this was impossible as the project was developed too late.

The researcher attended sessions of both sections of the course to be sure the inputs and atmosphere were similar. She performed a secondary analysis of the course evaluations administered at the conclusion of the course.

Analysis   Comparison of responses indicated that undergraduates believed they had gained more information than did the police recruits. While the police recruits learned from the course and decreased their prejudices, the amount of change did not equal that reported by the undergraduates. The researcher recognized the tentativeness of the results and qualified them with a consideration of the difference in entrance requirements to the course: it was mandatory for the police and elected by the undergraduates. The results are only suggestive and must be interpreted cautiously.

3. Suggestions for Police Field Projects

Study of the operation of a community's police force is more difficult than studying the other public service bureaucracies. The paramilitary nature of the police force requires secrecy for effective operation, making it awkward to investigate. The researcher may have to focus on interactions between policemen and citizens. This warning is not an absolute; some police departments are more open than others, allowing administration of questionnaires to members of the police force, and others even allowing tours of the police station and patrolling with policemen on duty.

Sample Topics

1. It may be possible to spend a day with a policeman on patrol. The observations provide insights into the police role from the policeman's point of view and reveal the variety of requests made of them in their work.

2. One might measure the differences in police patrol behavior in middle and lower-class areas through observation. He should notice how they are armed, how often they stop, how observant they are, who they tend to talk with or question.

3. One could use the Cumming et al. (1965) model of the three roles played by policemen as a framework for study. To see how prevalent the service role is, policemen might be asked how many babies they have delivered within a specified time period, how many cats rescued, how many accident victims aided, etc. The researcher could measure what proportion of police time is spent in each of the three roles. The policemen's opinions of activities in these roles could be compared—which one do policemen prefer to do, what do they dislike?

4. The policemen could be interviewed directly about their roles to determine how they feel about them. Do not focus on bringing out distressing material. Ask permission for such work.

5. One might gain permission to sit in a station house for several hours and obtain observation data on a police force's operation.

6. One might attend court sessions to see another aspect of the police role and the interactions in this setting.

7. A policeman on traffic duty is another setting for observing police operation. One should focus on the policeman's demeanor, his reactions to the categories of people he stops. A hospital emergency room is a stressful situation where policemen are frequently found in the course of their work.

8. The police recruitment sequence is interesting and shows the selection process at work in this bureaucracy. Documents detailing the steps required for entry into the police department are available.

E. SUPPLEMENTARY BIBLIOGRAPHY

Alex, Nicholas.
    1969   *Black in Blue: A Study of the Negro Policeman.* New York: Appleton.
American Behavioral Scientist.
    1968   "Urban violence and disorder." *American Behavioral Scientist* 2 (March-April).
            1-55.
Asinof, Eliot.
    1970   *People vs. Butcher.* New York: Viking.
Banton, Michael.
    1964   *The Policeman in the Community.* New York: Basic Books.

Bayley, David, and Harold Mendelsohn.
1969   *Minorities and the Police: Confrontation in America.* New York: Free Press.
Besag, Frank.
1967   *The Anatomy of a Riot.* Buffalo: State University at Buffalo Press.
Bittner, Egon.
1967   "The police on skid row: a study of peace-keeping." *American Sociological Review* 32 (October):699-715.
Black, Algernon.
1969   *The Police and the People.* New York: McGraw-Hill.
Blum, Richard (ed.).
1964   *Police Selection.* Springfield, Ill.: C. C. Thomas.
Bordua, David (ed.).
1967   *The Police: Six Sociological Essays.* New York: Wiley.
Bordua, David.
1968   "The police," pp. 174-181 in David L. Sills (ed.), *The Encyclopedia of the Social Sciences.* New York: Macmillan and Free Press, volume 12.
Bordua, David, and Albert J. Reiss, Jr.
1966   "Command, control, and charisma." *American Journal of Sociology* 72 (July): 68-76.
Bouma, Donald.
1970   *Kids and Cops: A Study in Mutual Hostility.* Grand Rapids, Mich.: Eerdmans.
Brim, Orville, and Stanton Wheeler.
1966   *Socialization After Childhood: Two Essays.* New York: Wiley.
Chevigny, Paul.
1969   *Police Power.* New York: Pantheon.
Cray, Edward.
1966   "Annotated bibliography on police review boards." *Law in Transition Quarterly* 3 (Summer):197-205.
1967   *The Big Blue Line: Police Versus Human Rights.* New York: Coward-McCann.
Cumming, Elaine, et al.
1965   "Policeman as philosopher, guide, and friend." *Social Problems* 12 (Winter):276-286.
Fogelson, Robert M.
1968   "From resentment to confrontation: the police, the Negroes, and the outbreak of the 1960's riots." *Political Science Quarterly* 83 (June):217-247.
Fogelson, Robert M. (ed.).
1971   *Police in America.* New York: Arno Press.
Fox, V.
1966   "Sociological and political aspects of police administration." *Sociology and Social Research* 51 (October):39-48.
Gellhorn, Walter.
1966   "Police review boards: hoax or hope." *Columbia University Forum* 9 (Summer): 4-10.
Germann, A. C.
1967   "Education and professional law enforcement." *Journal of Criminal Law, Criminology, and Police Science* 58 (December):603-609.
Haurek, E. W., and J. P. Clark.
1967   "Variants of the integration of social control agencies." *Social Problems* 15 (Summer):46-60.
Havlick, Robert.
1968   "Police recruit training." *Municipal Yearbook:* 339-350.
Hoffman, P.
1964   "Police Birchites: the blue backlash." *The Nation* 199 (December 7):425.

Hopkins, Ernest Jerome.
   1931   *Our Lawless Police.* New York: Viking.
Kates, Solis L.
   1950   "Rorshach responses, strong blank scales, and job satisfaction among police-
           men." *Journal of Applied Psychology* 34:249-54.
Kempton, Murray.
   1970   "Cops." *New York Review of Books* (November 5):3-7.
LaFave, Wayne.
   1965   *Arrest: the Decision to Take a Subject into Custody.* Boston: Little, Brown.
Matarazzo, Joseph.
   1964   "Characteristics of successful policemen and firemen applicants." *Journal of
           Applied Psychology* 48:123-133.
Mather, F. C.
   1959   *Public Order in the Age of the Chartists.* Manchester: The University Press.
The National Advisory Commission on Civil Disorders.
   1968   *Report of the National Advisory Commission on Civil Disorders.* New York:
           Dutton.
Neiderhoffer, Arthur.
   1967   *Behind the Shield: Police in the Urban Society.* Garden City, N.Y.: Doubleday.
Neiderhoffer, Arthur, and Abraham Blumberg (eds.).
   1970   *The Ambivalent Force: Perspective on the Police.* Boston: Ginn.
Osterburg, James.
   1967   "Cadet programs: an innovative change." *Journal of Criminal Law, Criminology,
           and Police Science* 58 (March):112-118.
Piliavin, Irving, and Scott Briar.
   1964   "Police encounters with juveniles." *American Journal of Sociology* 70 (Septem-
           ber):206-214.
Preiss, Jack, and Howard Ehrlich.
   1966   *An Examination of Role Theory: The Case of the State Police.* Lincoln: Univer-
           sity of Nebraska Press.
The President's Commission on Law Enforcement and the Administration of Justice.
   1967   *Task Force Report: The Police.* Washington, D.C.: United States Government
           Printing Office.
Ramsay, A. A. W.
   1938   *Sir Robert Peel.* New York: Dodd, Mead.
Reiss, Albert J., Jr.
   1968   "How common is police brutality?" *Trans*-action 8 (July-August):10-19.
Reith, Charles.
   1938   *The Police Idea: Its History and Evolution in England in the Eighteenth Century
           and After.* London: Oxford University Press.
Richardson, James.
   1970   *The New York Police: Colonial Times to 1901.* New York: Oxford University
           Press.
Saunders, Charles B., Jr.
   1970   *Upgrading the American Police: Education and Training for Better Law Enforce-
           ment.* Washington, D.C.: The Brookings Institution.
Sayre, N.
   1967   "College for policemen." *New Statesman* 73 (May):608.
Schulz, David.
   1968   "Some aspects of the policeman's role as it impinges upon family life in a Negro
           ghetto." Paper presented to the American Sociological Association meetings,
           Boston, Massachusetts (August).

Shekow, R., and D. V. Roemer.
1966   "Riot that did not happen." *Social Problems* 14 (Fall):221-233.
Skolnick, Jerome.
1966   *Justice Without Trial*. New York: Wiley.
1969   *The Politics of Protest*. New York: Simon & Schuster.
Smith, Ralph.
1965   *The Tarnished Badge*. New York: T. Y. Crowell.
Stern, Mort.
1962   "What makes policemen go wrong." *Journal of Criminal Law, Criminology, and Police Science* 53 (March):97-101.
Stinchcombe, A. L.
1963   "Institutions of privacy in the determination of police administrative practices." *American Journal of Sociology* 69 (September):150-160.
Terris, Bruce.
1967   "The role of police." *Annals* 374 (November):58-69.
Walker, Daniel.
1968   *Rights in Conflict: The Violent Confrontation of Demonstrators and Police in the Parks and Streets of Chicago During the Week of the Democratic National Convention of 1968*. New York: Dutton.
Walsh, James Leo.
1969   "The professional cop." Paper presented to the American Sociological Association meetings, San Francisco, California (September 1-4).
Westley, William A.
1951   *The Police: A Sociological Study of Law, Custom and Morality*. University of Chicago. Unpublished doctoral dissertation.
1953   "Violence and the police." *American Journal of Sociology* 59 (July):34-41.
1956   "Secrecy and the police." *Social Forces* 34 (March):254-257.
Whittemore, L. H.
1969   *Cop! A Close-Up of Violence and Tragedy*. New York: Holt, Rinehart & Winston.
Wilson, James Q.
1963   "The police and their problems: a theory." *Public Policy* 12:189-216.
1964   "Generational and ethnic differences among career police officers." *American Journal of Sociology* 69 (March):522-528.
1968   *Varieties of Police Behavior*. Cambridge: Harvard University Press.
Wood, S. M.
1966   "Uniform: its significance as a factor in role relationships." *Sociological Review* n.s. 14 (June):139-151.

5

Public welfare

A. INTRODUCTION

In Chapter 5 we discuss the contemporary public service bureaucracy known as public welfare. Section B presents general sociological concepts applicable to public welfare. In Section C these concepts are used to understand the structure and operation of public welfare. Section D includes a variety of field projects about welfare, largely drawn from previously completed projects. The format of Section D has three subsections similar to those in Chapters 3 and 4. Section E is a supplementary bibliography offering sources of additional information helpful to people investigating public welfare in depth.

B. CONCEPTS

1. Social Support

A public welfare bureaucracy provides social support to people within the community in which it is located. Social support is the service's primary purpose, corresponding to the police provision of social control and the schools' offering of socialization. Social support is really assistance concerning employability and shelter. Most public welfare bureaucracies offer several types of help; financial, advisory, and referral. The social support provided assists people burdened with problems or lacking resources and being unable to take care of and provide for themselves. Sickness, injury, death, separation, divorce, or unemployment may lessen a family's income, psychological motivation, and capacity to cope. Through social workers and money allotments, public welfare lessens a person's suffering and hardship.

In earlier periods of history, troubled people looked to relatives for help and assistance. People lived either with or near many relatives, so that in emergencies they could take over and provide necessary help as substitution for employment and housing. To them, care of another person or two was not a problem, especially in farming communities where extra help was always useful.

While today relatives remain a major source of help in periods of trouble, changes have occurred that make it more difficult for relatives to help as efficiently and painlessly as in previous periods, one reason being that many people no longer live in the immediate vicinity of their relatives. Also very few people

54

depend wholly or partially on farming; most people live in households dependent on the wages or salary of one person. This limited flow of resources into a family makes it financially difficult for relatives to aid one another. Most families live in apartments or small one-family homes, and these housing arrangements lack extra space in which to fit a relative with marital or economic troubles. Residences used to have more flexibility; farmhouses and rambling houses always seemed to have the possibility of creating an extra room or suite, not because they were larger but because the rooms were used for multiple purposes when necessary.

Geographic, economic, and housing changes limit the ability of contemporary families to harbor and support relatives in trouble. The current plight of elderly Americans illustrates this problem very clearly. Older people used to live with relatives, their children, and their families. This arrangement was mutually beneficial; grandparents helped the harried parents with childcare and housework, while the parents cared for the grandparents' financial and emotional needs. Due to the three changes previously mentioned, grandparents today are less likely to live with their children. Instead they retire to small apartments, rooming houses, and nursing homes to live lonely, empty lives. Public welfare bureaucracies are increasingly involved with providing financial and psychological services for the aged. The unmarried person, the separated or divorced mother with children, and the unemployed person are other categories of people increasingly reliant on public welfare rather than relatives.

The sight of starving, homeless, suffering people would offend and upset all members of a community. Large numbers of these people, with no means of assistance, would be disruptive to the functioning of our complex and interdependent communities. Widespread illness, plagues, crime, and violence would violently intrude upon the lives of everyone. The interfering, interruptive potential of these unfortunate people demands that the community confront these problems. Impersonal, formalized procedures called public welfare agencies, social work services, and settlement houses have been established to handle and solve these human problems. As the number and variety of these problems have grown, so have the number and size of the formal organizations mandated to deal with them.

2. The Poor

Public welfare agencies differ from the police and the schools in that they work principally with the poor, and in this sense Beck (1967) calls public welfare an extraordinary system. It is a community institution chartered for the care of a situation defined as a supplementary or special case in the community. One might conclude from this that public welfare as currently structured could never handle a widespread condition of the society such as massive, long-term unemployment.

The poor do not have the resources of the majority of the members of their society, although this does not necessarily mean that they lack only money. If we accept an economic definition of the poor, the entire population of the United

States would appear to be wealthy, with a per capita income that is high in relation to the underdeveloped countries of the world. When we look at the large increase in wages in the United States during this century, it would seem that the poor must no longer exist. Despite these indications, however, the welfare lists are growing very fast.

The economic definition of poverty does not properly define the poor. As Coser (1965) argues, the social definition of the poor is most important—people are poor because they are defined as poor. A graduate student living on $2,000 a year is not considered to be poor, but an underemployed man earning $2,000 a year definitely is. The difference between these two people with similar economic assets lies in their lifestyles. While the graduate student has a future orientation, viewing his current poverty as a temporary and even necessary step in actualizing his ambitions, the underemployed man has a present orientation, seeing no end to his condition, living and acting as if it is his perpetual fate.

Accepting assistance from public welfare agencies is a visible and public acknowledgement of oneself as poor. The graduate student probably would not apply for public welfare, whereas the underemployed man is more likely to do so. There are many people scrimping and managing on an extremely small amount of money who do not consider themselves poor and would not seek public welfare assistance. The classification of being poor is not an economic absolute; in the eyes of the rest of the society, it is a relative phenomenon.

3. Stigma and Dependency

Being stigmatized—marked off visibly from the rest of the community and from normal social relationships—is a corollary of being defined as poor and receiving public welfare. Coser (1965) states that throughout history the poor have been set apart in society, and that this is generally visibly manifested in their separate living areas. In ancient cities the poor lived just outside the town walls; today the poor live huddled together in ghettos, slums, and inner-city areas.

There is a functional reason why all societies classify the poor and force them to live in visible, well-defined areas. By pointing out the misery and misfortune of the poor, the society can establish by contrast the normative standards of the good life. Just as criminals receive punishment for its reinforcement value to remind others of the established laws, the poor suffer poverty to remind others of the value of the culturally valued lifestyle.

This functional phenomenon has particular importance for modern life. Max Weber's discussion of the Protestant Ethic shows that work is a means by which modern man believes he can determine his eternal destiny. Economic success leads to eternal reward in heaven, about which there is no definite information available. While work has connotations of religious salvation and psychological self-identification, it has been increasingly rationalized and segmented and therefore lacks intrinsic reward. Conversely the Protestant Ethic assigns unproductive people to eternal damnation and holds that their receiving charity would be tampering with God's preordained nature of things. The stingy, punitive, restrictive tone of today's public welfare programs stems from the intellectual heritage of the Protestant Ethic and its positive valuation of work.

From the ideas of the Protestant Ethic we associate being poor with being sinful, outcast, or stigmatized. The tone of moral failure associated with the status of being poor has created the stingy and suspicious orientation of public welfare programs. Protestant Ethic ideology associates poverty with personal failure, destroying any reason for providing extensive help to the poor. The poor carry the stigma of failure and rejection.

When the poor are viewed in this way, receiving aid cannot be considered a reciprocal exchange between equals. They are in a dependent position and can receive assistance only because they are seen as unable to offer anything in return. Coser (1965) discusses the social structure in which public welfare is provided and which engenders feelings of dependency. Social relationships between equals involve mutual giving and receiving. This relationship is truncated when the poor are involved, because they must receive public welfare without being able to give in return.

Receiving a subsidy does not in itself make someone dependent. Farmers receive assistance, workers receive unemployment compensation, homeowners can offset interest payments on their mortgages, businessmen have tax deductions and benefits—these classes of people are not considered dependent. As forms of delayed compensation for service to the community, these subsidies are not available to welfare recipients because they do not productively contribute to society.

The social structure of public welfare stigmatizes the poor, placing them outside the realm of social exchange. Making them negative examples for the rest of society by defining them as nonproductive creates their inherent dependency. Ironically stigmatization and dependency contribute to the often-criticized apathetic nature of the poor. Evaluation by others is the strongest molder of one's self-image, and the poor develop negative self-images as a result of the society's response to them. The current emphasis on the welfare recipient's need to work is an attempt to institute reciprocity between the welfare recipient and the rest of society.

4. Welfare as a Right

When organized and given by the community's more successful members to poor people who are considered to be undeserving and failures, public welfare is a charity. It is a result of the generosity of others, and the poor should not expect it. This orientation has dominated public welfare programs in the United States.

In the late nineteenth century Western European countries developed another understanding of public welfare, a viewpoint just now beginning to be discussed in the United States. At that time in Europe, the idea grew in popularity that all citizens had rights to adequate income, education, and health care, contradicting the earlier notion that these services were given out of charity and were provided inadequately or sometimes not at all. The key to this new ideology is the concept of the citizen as a member of a separate, politically organized society.

This new concept of a right to welfare recognizes society's need for healthy, educated citizens capable of operating at maximum potential. It is in the society's best interest to guarantee basic minimal conditions of life for all citizens. This concept could not really affect the United States until the flood of free immigration of new members was brought under control. Appearing in the United States initially in the New Deal programs of Social Security and the Works Progress Administration the idea is now gaining notice in such diverse areas of communication as the National Welfare Rights Organization, the Nixon revision of public welfare called the Family Assistance Plan, and the guidelines of the Economic Opportunity Act. Welfare as a right and not a charity is championed by liberal politicians concerned with social welfare and even some conservative economists. This increasing awareness is also due to the activities of the organizations of welfare recipients. Although it is a long step from awareness to acceptance, the process of change has begun.

5. Social Workers as Missionaries

Each person who applies for public welfare is classified as a case and assigned to a social worker who tries to counsel him, make application, and certify eligibility for financial aid. The casework model around which public welfare is organized is derived from Freudian psychiatry, which emphasizes the helpfulness of verbalizing problems and emotional conflicts. But there is great irony in the present organization. The social setting of Freudian psychiatry was devised to help middle class patients with emotional troubles confront deeply repressed issues through verbalization of the unresolved conflicts. The public welfare recipient is a victim of deficient resources and impoverished social situations. His plight is the result of many factors: poor housing, inadequate food, lack of available jobs, and bad schools. Discussing problems with a welfare worker, as the middle class neurotic does with his therapist, has no effect on the real sources of his problems, which are in the society and not in the client. Silberman (1964) argues strongly that this misuse of the Freudian casework approach has had little or no effect on the problems of public welfare recipients.

The public welfare social worker's lifestyle hinders his effectiveness. He has worked hard to achieve his secure, relatively well-paid job and believes that such opportunities as he has had are available to all public welfare clients if they would follow a similar life pattern. Because of his desire to introduce his clients to these ambitions, in this sense we call social work "missionary". He holds out a model which if followed precisely will lead his clients one by one to the contributing life of full membership in society.

This world view emphasizing hard work and respectful demeanor was the ethos of the successful immigrants in the early twentieth century. Much has changed since then; steady work in blue collar and unskilled positions has decreased, skin color which is irradicable marks off the ghetto dweller from the rest of the society, and education and skill are needed to compete in the current job market. The structural conditions of society have changed so much that proper attitudes and eagerness for hard work do not guarantee movement from a slum into the achieving society. The emphasis of public welfare social work on individual attitudes is outdated.

Some public welfare social workers are adopting a client advocate position. Rather than work to increase mobility for individual clients into the larger society, they try to improve conditions of life for those receiving welfare. The social worker as client advocate makes sure the client receives all aid to which he is legally entitled without first determining his moral worthiness. Other people and organizations are also helping the client face up to and demand available but hidden rights.

C. CONCEPT CLARIFICATION PROJECTS

The following concepts integrate your personal insights and experiences with the new information gained from the readings here and in *Social Change in Urban America.*

Questions Requiring Short Paragraph Answers

1. a. What is social support? Give some examples from your own experiences.
   b. Public welfare provides social support to community members. What are other sources of social support?
   c. Why are relatives the most frequently used and often the best source of social support?
   d. Are social support services always necessary?

2. a. Do you think the lifestyle of the poor differs so much from that of other members of society that poverty could be considered a culture?
   b. Describe the lifestyle of the poor. How does it differ from that of the middle class?
   c. Some people say that it is impossible for lower class people to organize themselves into action groups. What do you think and why?
   d. Are economic criteria the best definitions of poverty? Why? Why not?

3. a. Why are the poor often described in negative terms? What does this represent?
   b. In what ways do the poor serve the same function for society as criminals?
   c. How does stigmatization work?
   d. Have attitudes towards the poor influenced the operation of public welfare programs?

4. a. Why do public welfare programs have social work services while unemployment compensation programs are administered impersonally?
   b. Why should welfare recipients be looked down on while public welfare is only one of the government subsidy programs that include farm, homebuilding, and small business subsidies?
   c. Social exchange proceeds most easily between equals. What are the social consequences of placing the poor in dependent positions?

    d. What are the psychological consequences for a person in a dependent position?

5. a. What is the sociological significance of receiving something as charity? as a right?

    b. What are the reasons for the restrictive attitudes towards welfare? For example the United States spends the smallest percent of the tax dollar on welfare of any modern western nation.

6. a. What are the consequences of the Freudian influence on social work?

    b. Do you think an emphasis on personal adjustment will help solve the problems causing people to seek public welfare?

    c. How does the public welfare social worker see himself and his profession? What are his goals?

    d. What are some alternative ways to administer welfare?

Summary Questions

    The following topics require more thought and more detail. Think carefully about the multiple interpretations possible and prepare an encompassing answer.

1. Comment on the following quotation: "The notion that. . .poverty is a penalty for laziness, error, or failure persists as an almost unconscious hangover of attitudes conditioned by a wholly different set of economic facts." The author is Wilbur Cohen, and the statement was included in William Moore's book, *The Vertical Ghetto*, New York: Random House, 1969.

2. Social life is socially constructed, as a result of shared and revised interpretations. What consequences does this have for the poor?

3. Are the poor an inevitable and/or necessary group in society?

4. Would redefinition of eligibility for public welfare have repercussions for the definition of work? If so, what would the repercussions be?

5. What are the positive and negative consequences of providing social work assistance in the public welfare program? What alternatives are possible?

D. EXAMPLES OF PUBLIC WELFARE FIELD PROJECTS

1. A Detailed Example of a Public Welfare Field Project

    The Problem   Several persons were interested in recently developed organizations of public welfare clients, which lobby and demonstrate to improve life conditions and benefits. These organizations appeared in the latter half of the 1960's.

    There is a prevailing belief that poor people are unable to organize themselves to act for desired changes, but organizations of public welfare clients refute this opinion. The researchers wanted to see if these public welfare organizations were organizations of the poor, and, if so, what fostered organizational interests. They realized the need to understand the source and composition of these organizations to predict their potential for future growth and influence. They were also interested in specifying the motivations of the members; their goals, tactics, and attitudes.

    Background on the operation of public welfare shows why mass outbursts can influence change. Public welfare is the legal right of any eligible citizen, and because of the volume of work and large numbers of people affected, it is administered by bureaucracies. The individual must confront the public welfare bureaucracy in any exchange, and these interactions are influenced by imbalance in size and power. Just as the American workers had to join together in labor unions to effectively confront big business, public welfare clients recognize their need to join together to obtain comparability in size for effective negotiations. Individuals or small groups of individuals cannot confront a large impersonal bureaucracy. They must band together in a sizeable way to communicate effectively with large-scale structures.

The researchers were interested in a local public welfare clients' group and the emerging national organization. The simultaneous appearance of the two groups raised interesting questions of comparison and contrast. Were there differences between them, and if so, what were they and what did they mean? Evaluation of the two public welfare clients' organizations was a major focus for the field project.

The Hypothesis   This project explored the origins and interrelationships of the newly emerged welfare clients' organizations. The researchers began with the contention that the local clients were a community group protesting against the local welfare bureaucracy. With some investigation they realized the local clients did more than protest injustices; they also lobbied for the rights of citizens receiving welfare. The initial description of the public welfare clients' organization, a group protesting unfair treatment, was inadequate. The clients tried an ideological change, insisting that they had rights or legitimate demands. They expanded their problem to state that local and national organizations protest against the welfare bureaucracy and seek rights for welfare clients. This problem statement served as a guide for collecting information about public welfare clients' protest organizations.

Data Collection   The researchers used a variety of methods to gather information. They constructed an interview schedule to guide conversations with members of the local and national welfare clients' organizations. Interviews were supplemented with reading and content analysis of the organizations' publications. They obtained respondents with the "snow-ball" technique, asking respondents to name others willing to participate in the study. They interviewed twelve members of the local and national clients' organizations.

Analysis   They found that both organizations originated through the efforts of a nonclient. The local agency developed from the disgust of a public welfare social worker who left her job to organize clients. The national organization gained a local following through the efforts of an organizer sent to the area to involve the grassroots and create a local branch of the national organization. He did this by leafletting at supermarkets, contacting clergy, and door-to-door canvassing.

The two organizations differed considerably. The local group of welfare clients cared primarily about immediate, material benefits. They had conservative opinions about the existing welfare bureaucracy and believed eligibility checking was necessary and should be done more efficiently to make the welfare worker more aware of the client's real needs. This group had a very informal structure, the office being casually staffed by the clients themselves who often had to bring their children with them. The members felt that the sporadic quality of their communication decreased their effectiveness.

The researchers felt that the informality of the local client organization also limited its effectiveness. It relied on intermittent dramatic action and nonviolent demonstrations. Most members believed change through legal channels was most desirable, but their informal structure precluded sustained action and success with their campaigns. Feeling hurt and irritated by the way the welfare bureaucracy treated them, they wanted more respect. They specifically mentioned the public welfare social worker's attitude toward them and stressed their need for adequate self-images.

The national organization had a better-developed, more coherent strategy, emphasizing that public welfare programs, policies, and laws are products of the local, state, and federal levels of government. Action to change them must be carried out on all three levels. It sought to develop massive grassroots support for political influence.

The local branch of the national organization had much more structure. The organizer structured the group carefully and established definite operating procedures, including selecting specific issues about which to challenge the welfare bureaucracy for change. If they did not see the desired changes, they were willing to behave disruptively. The organizer became less visible, allowing the clients to feel they ran the operation, while he remained in the background skillfully structuring and guiding actions.

There were interorganizational conflicts. The indigenous organization felt outsmarted and thought that the other clients were being manipulated by an outsider. They refused to join with the branch organization because of differences in goals, tactics, and a resentment of their efficiency and competence. The members of the indigenous organization felt the branch organization was hurting their cause by its negative publicity. The researchers believed the national organization was gaining strength locally and perceived that it would override the indigenous organization which would then become an even more diffuse structure.

This research provided a description of the birth of a grassroots organization. These organizations had disputes in their initial stages, and these stages give clues to the real meaning of the subsequent organization that appeared to the public in its mature form.

2. Other Examples of Public Welfare Field Projects

a. Anomie in public welfare social workers and its consequences

The Problem   One person wanted to measure attitudes of public welfare social workers and determine if they influenced their perception of their clients. Neiderhoffer (1967) showed that time in service increases police cynicism; the same phenomenon may happen to public welfare social workers. The researcher decided to see if differences in attitudes had consequences for job definitions and differing perceptions of the welfare client.

The Hypothesis   There are two hypotheses in this project. The anomie level of the public welfare social worker is directly related to length of time in service. The more anomic the public welfare social worker, the more negative he is towards welfare clients.

Data Collection   The researcher used the Srole Anomie Scale to measure the social worker's attitudes. This scale has been widely used to measure despair, fatalism, and alienation. The version in current use contains five sentences to which the respondent reacts using fixed response categories, such as strongly agree, agree, disagree, strongly disagree. He measured the client's perceptions with two statements constructed with response categories similar to the anomie scale, to maintain a consistent style in the one-page questionnaire. The two items about clients asked the welfare worker to evaluate how needy most of the clients on her caseload were and whether the current welfare payment structure was equitable and adequate according to her experience.

Analysis   Creating a 2x2 table with the variables high and low anomie, less than five years of service in public welfare and more than five years of service, the researcher reported that the distribution was statistically significant at the .05 level using a chi-square test. Amount of years in service increased the worker's level of anomie, similar to the increased cynicism Neiderhoffer (1967) reported among long-term policemen.

Creating another 2x2 table with the variables high and low levels of anomie and attitudes towards the welfare client, sympathetic or punitive, the researcher reported that this distribution was statistically significant at the .05 level using the chi-square test. The social worker's level of anomie was related to the punitiveness of his attitude toward the client.

People working in a bureaucracy reflect change in attitudes as a result of their experiences within the organization. The number of subjects was too small to be other than suggestive, but the frustration and annoyance caused by welfare programs seem to have had a negative effect on the social worker's view of his work.

b. Public welfare social workers and public welfare clients:
a comparison of responses

The Problem   Three persons were interested in the degree of congruence between public welfare social workers' and clients' attitudes towards welfare and its place in the community. They felt that investigation and specification of these attitudes was important in planning program improvement.

The Hypothesis   This exploratory project sought information on public welfare clients' and social workers' attitudes towards the philosophy of welfare, the role of the public welfare social worker, operation of the public welfare program, and the neediness of welfare clients.

Data Collection   They located their research in a poor, rundown, middle-sized city in a metropolitan area. Responding clients were obtained through trial and error, door-to-door canvassing, and referrals from other respondents. They used an informal, open-ended interview schedule and had a general conversation with their fifteen respondents. They also interviewed several public welfare personnel—supervisors and social workers—using a similar interview schedule. The parallel interview system was used to obtain data on the four foci of the project.

Analysis   Most clients said welfare did not pay enough to live on and thought the amount should be increased by $10 per week. Interestingly, one-quarter of the clients thought receiving welfare should have obligations attached to it such as accepting work, but one-half felt no obligation. Most wanted more regular visits from the social worker and reported receiving very few. The clients were conservative in their comments on welfare programs and had few ideas about possible changes.

The public welfare social workers and supervisors strongly resisted cooperating with the researchers. Three interviews were conducted outside the office. The social workers had been on the job a short time and all were planning to leave in the near future. They felt the caseload was too large, the salary too low, that clients should have a part in determining their budgets, and that clients should not be visited regularly.

There are several areas of difference between clients and personnel. Welfare clients see the welfare office as a possible source of work, but the social workers see it as only a referral center. Clients are more interested than the social worker in home visits from their counselor. The social workers think the clients should determine their level of payment, but the client does not. The clients were passive and conservative, but the welfare worker has a different view of them.

c. Public welfare social work and the concept of the culture of poverty

The Problem   The phrase "culture of poverty" is commonly used to describe an excuse for the existence of poverty and its apparently nonproductive lifestyle. People look at the negative characteristics of the poor and say they are the results of the culture of poverty. This explains nothing; the poor exist within the society and are integrally related to it. One person was concerned with the influence of the culture of poverty ideology and wanted to measure how prevalent it was among public welfare social workers.

The Hypothesis   This project was exploratory and measured the prevalence of the culture of poverty ideology among public welfare social workers.

Data Collection   The researcher constructed a short questionnaire about causes of poverty, possible solutions, and aims of a public welfare social worker's role. The questionnaire was organized around a statement and possible responses reflecting approaches to poverty, including several using the culture of poverty. The questionnaire was given to public welfare social workers in several different local offices, selected by their willingness to participate.

Analysis   The idea of a culture of poverty was prevalent among welfare workers. The respondents most frequently mentioned causes of poverty based on individual deficiencies. They emphasized individual resocialization as the best cure for poverty and saw themselves as resocialization models. While the workers with more years of service were more likely to emphasize individual resocialization as a remedy for poverty, the less-experienced social workers mentioned institutional methods.

Perhaps the nature of public welfare social work had a selective effect on the responses. A person who sees poverty as an institutional or societal problem would not work in a public welfare bureaucracy, but rather in a helping organization with an orientation more congruent with his beliefs.

d. The effectiveness of communication from public welfare departments

The Problem   One person was concerned about the misinformation and misperceptions that characterize public welfare programs.

The Hypothesis   This was an exploratory project investigating the degree of misinformation or lack of information made available to public welfare clients and the general public.

Data Collection   The project used a variety of information sources; participant observation, analyses of published materials, and unstructured interviews. Posing as a potential client, the researcher tried to obtain explanatory material from a public welfare office. It was impossible to obtain eligibility requirements, general departmental regulations, an application for welfare, or published sources of information that the bureaucracy acknowledged but never showed.

Analysis   Trying to view public welfare through the eyes of a potential client and the general public, the researcher found the program to be uncommunicative. The welfare office he visited posted no information in the waiting room, and he was told that most clients have no need for such information. Personal contacts with public welfare social workers were cordial, but there remained problems of information transmission. It may be that the national welfare clients' organization serves a real need in making information more available to the client and the potential client about the operation of public welfare and the available programs.

The researcher also conducted an informal park bench survey of the general public's information about welfare. This haphazard information collection from working people further supported the idea that gaps exist in the public's knowledge of welfare programs. The public's and the clients' lack of information about welfare contributes to the continuation of welfare's negative connotations. Effective change requires better communication with all members of the community.

3. Suggestions for Public Welfare Field Projects

There are two broad categories of projects in public welfare. The first deals with questions of policy or attitudes, and the second considers how actual welfare field operations are carried out and whether these confirm official policy statements. In investigating field operations the attitudes and values of the welfare recipient are a prime focus of interest.

Policy questions can be approached through analysis of newspapers and other mass media accounts of issues and programs. Interviews with people charged with direction of welfare programs—the director of a settlement house, for example—yields significant data on how professionals see and interpret official policy. Moreover the degree to which personal value systems influence these perceptions and behavior patterns may become apparent.

The second type of project is designed to determine what is the actual operation of public welfare programs. One way to assess the program is to obtain two sets of responses, from welfare administrators stating what their programs are doing, and from clients to see if what they say is actually being done. Two groups of researchers could work out the series of interviews or questionnaires necessary to reveal the dual perspective on the process. The duality is valuable because more dimensions of reality are uncovered by this duality, which facilitates better analyses.

Sample Topics

1. A project on policy formulation might examine the ideological orientation implicit or explicit in policy directives. Is welfare a necessity? A burden? An act of charity? A right? Some predictions of social change could arise from such a study.

2. What are the community members' opinions on specific social issues such as illegitimacy, compulsory birth control for welfare mothers, and compulsory sterilization. These questions should focus on the most relevant, topical, and controversial issues in a particular community.

3. Possibilities for change in welfare policies might be predicted from the attitudes of dominant ethnic groups. How do they differ from those of welfare recipients?

4. The current recommendations for improving the public welfare program can be compared and contrasted with each other and with the existing program.

5. The aged are an increasingly large problem in American society. One could examine provisions made for the aged in current programs and consider if they are adequately covered.

6. A job always influences the person who holds it. One person could find out about the training a public welfare social worker undergoes upon entering the role, as well as the recruitment process used. He could consider the consequences recruitment processes and training have for the person who occupies the role.

7. Some people might be interested in comprehensive studies of the welfare programs available locally for categories of people such as children and unemployed fathers.

E. SUPPLEMENTARY BIBLIOGRAPHY

Ad Hoc Committee on Advocacy.
 1969   "The social worker as advocate." *Social Work* 14 (April):16-23.
Anderson, C. L.
 1967   "Preliminary study of generational economic dependency." *Social Forces* 45 (June):516-520.
Barr, Sherman.
 1965   "Budgeting and the poor." *Public Welfare* 23 (October):246-250.
Beck, Bernard.
 1967   "Welfare as a moral category." *Social Problems* 14 (Winter):258-277.

Blau, Peter.
1960 "Orientation towards clients in a public welfare agency." *Administrative Science Quarterly* 3 (December):341-361.
Bowen, D. R., et al.
1968 "Deprivation, mobility, and orientation toward protest of the urban poor." *American Behavioral Scientist* 11 (March):20-24.
Brager, George.
1963 "Organizing the unaffiliated in a low-income area." *Social Work* 3 (April):34-40.
1968 "Advocacy and political behavior." *Social Work* 13 (April):5-15.
Brager, George, and Francis Purcell (eds.).
1967 *Community Action Versus Poverty: Readings from the Mobilization Experience.* New Haven: College and University Press.
Brehm, C. T., and T. R. Savino.
1964 "Demand for general assistance payments." *American Economic Review* 54 (December):1002-1018.
Briggs, Asa.
1961 "Welfare statement in historical perspective." *European Journal of Sociology* 2:221-258.
Burgess, Elaine.
1965 "Poverty and dependency: some selected characteristics." *Journal of Social Issues* 21 (January):79-97.
Burns, Eveline.
1965 "Where welfare falls short." *The Public Interest* 1 (Fall):82-95.
Caplowitz, David.
1967 *The Poor Pay More: Consumer Practices of Low Income Families.* New York: Free Press.
Cloward, Richard, and Richard Elman.
1966 "Advocacy in the ghetto." *Trans*-action 3 (December):27-35.
Cloward, Richard, and Irwin Epstein.
1965 "Private social welfare's disengagement from the poor," in *Proceedings of Annual Social Work Day Institute.* School of Social Welfare. New York State University at Buffalo (May).
Cloward, Richard, and Frances Fox Piven.
1966 "The weight of the poor: a strategy to end poverty." *The Nation* 202 (May 2): 510-517.
1967a "The weapon of poverty: birth of a movement." *The Nation* 204 (May 8):582-586.
1967b "We've got rights: the no-longer silent welfare poor." *New Republic* (August 5): 23-27.
1968a "Migration, politics, and welfare." *Saturday Review* 51 (November 16):31-35.
1968b "Workers and welfare: the poor against themselves" *The Nation* 207 (November 25):558-562.
Cohen, Albert K., and Harold Hodges.
1963 "Characteristics of the lower blue collar class." *Social Problems* 10 (Spring):303-334.
Cohen, Nathan E.
1968 *Social Work in the American Tradition.* New York: Holt, Rinehart & Winston.
Coser, Lewis.
1965 "The sociology of poverty." *Social Problems* 13 (Fall):140-148.
Donovan, John C.
1967 *The Politics of Poverty.* New York: Western.

Eisman, Martin.
  1969   "Social work's new role in the welfare class revolution." *Social Work* 14 (April):
          80-86.
Elman, Richard.
  1966   *The Poorhouse State*. New York: Dell.
Ferman, Louis, et al. (ed.).
  1965   *Poverty in America*. Ann Arbor: University of Michigan Press.
Gilbert, G. E.
  1966   "Policymaking in public welfare: the 1962 amendments." *Political Science Quar-
          terly* 81 (June):196-224.
Gordon, M.
  1967   "Social security and welfare: dynamic stagnation." *Public Administration Re-
          view* 27 (March):87-90.
Gordon, Margaret S. (ed.).
  1965   *Poverty in America*. San Francisco: Chandler.
Green, A. D.
  1966   "The professional social worker in the bureaucracy." *Social Service Review* 40
          (March):71-83.
Haber, Alan.
  1967   "The American underclass." *Poverty and Human Resources Abstracts* 2 (May-
          June):5-19.
Harrington, Michael.
  1962   *The Other America*. Baltimore: Penguin.
Hoshino, G.
  1967   "Simplification of the means test and its consequences." *Social Service Review*
          41 (September):237-249.
Howard, Donald S.
  1969   *Social Welfare: Values, Means, and Ends*. New York: Random House.
Irelan, Lola M., and Arthur Besner.
  1965   "Low income outlook on life." *Welfare in Review* 3 (September):13-19.
Jacobs, Glenn.
  1968   "The reification of the notion of subculture in public welfare." *Social Casework*
          49 (November):527-534.
Jeffers, Camille.
  1967   *Living Poor*. Ann Arbor, Michigan: Ann Arbor Publishing.
Kahn, Gerald, and Ellen Perkins.
  1964   "Families receiving A.F.D.C.: what do they have to live on." *Welfare in Review*
          2 (October):7-15.
Kolack, Shirley.
  1968   "Study of status inconsistency among social work professionals." *Social Prob-
          lems* 15 (Winter):365-376.
Leacock, E.
  1968   "Distortions of working class reality in American social science." *Science and
          Society* 31 (Winter):1-21. Reply by Lee Rainwater, 32 (Winter 1968):80-88.
LeBeaux, Charles.
  1963   "Life in A.D.C.: budget of despair." *New University Thought* 3:26-35.
Levens, Helene.
  1968   "Organizational affiliation and powerlessness: a case study of the welfare poor."
          Social Problems 16 (Summer):18-32.
Liebow, Eliot.
  1967   *Tally's Corner*. Boston: Little, Brown.

Maas, Henry (ed.).
1964   *Five Fields of Social Service*. New York: National Association of Social Workers.
Marshall, Thomas H.
1965   *Class, Citizenship, and Social Class*. Garden City, N.Y.: Doubleday.
Meissner, Hanna (ed.).
1966   *Poverty in the Affluent Society*. New York: Harper & Row.
Miller, Herman P.
1965   *Rich Man, Poor Man*. New York: New American Library.
Miller, S. M., and Martin Rein.
1966   "Inequality and policy," pp. 426-516 in Howard S. Becker (ed.), *Social Problems.* New York: Wiley.
Miller, S. M., and Frank Riessman.
1968   *Social Class and Social Policy*. New York: Basic Books.
Miller, William B.
1959   "Implications of urban lower class culture for social work." *Social Service Review* 33 (September):219-236.
Moynihan, Daniel P. (ed.).
1969   *On Understanding Poverty: Perspectives for the Social Sciences.* New York: Basic Books.
Moynihan, Daniel P.
1965   "The professionalization of reform." *The Public Interest* 1 (Fall):6-16.
1968   "The crisis in welfare." *The Public Interest* 10 (Winter):3-29.
Mugge, Robert H.
1965   "Aide to families with dependent children: initial findings of the 1961 report on the characteristics of the recipients." *Social Security Bulletin* 26 (March):3-15.
Pauley, R. M.
1966   "Public welfare agency of the future." *Social Casework* 47 (May):286-292.
Piven, Frances Fox, and Richard Cloward.
1967   "Rent strike: disrupting the slum system." *New Republic* 157 (December 2):11-15.
1968   "Dissensus politics: a strategy for winning economic rights." *New Republic* 158 (April 20):20-24.
Rainwater, Lee.
1960   *And the Poor Get Children*. Chicago: Quadrangle.
Rainwater, Lee, and William Yancey.
1967   *The Moynihan Report and the Politics of Controversy*. Cambridge: M.I.T. Press.
Rein, Martin.
1965   "The strange case of public dependency." *Trans*-action 2 (December):15-23.
Schlesinger, Benjamin.
1966   *Poverty in Canada and the United States*. Toronto: University of Toronto Press.
Schneiderman, Leonard.
1964   "Value orientation preferences of chronic relief recipients." *Social Work* 9 (July): 13-18.
Schorr, Alvin.
1964a   "The non-culture of poverty." *American Journal of Ortho-Psychiatry* 34 (October):907-912.
1964b   *Slums and Social Insecurity*. Washington, D.C.: United States Government Printing Office.
1966a   "Against a negative income tax." *The Public Interest* 5 (Fall):110-117.
1966b   *Poor Kids*. New York: Basic Books.
1968   *Explorations in Social Policy*. New York: Basic Books.

Schwartz, Jerome, and Milton Chernin.
1967 "Participation of recipients in public welfare planning and administration." *Social Service Review* 41 (March):10-22.
Scott, R. A.
1967 "Selection of clients by the social welfare agencies: the case of the blind." *Social Problems* 14 (Winter):248-257.
Shannon, Lyle W.
1963 "The public's perception of social welfare agencies and organizations in an industrial community." *Journal of Negro Education* 32 (Summer):276-285.
Silberman, Charles.
1964 *Crisis in Black and White.* New York: Random House.
Simmel, Georg.
1965 "The poor." *Social Problems* 13 (Fall):110-140.
Stein, Bruno.
1971 *On Relief.* New York: Basic Books
Steiner, Gilbert.
1966 *Social Insecurity: The politics of Welfare.* Skokie, Ill.: Rand McNally.
1971 *The State of Welfare.* Washington, D.C.: The Brookings Institution.
Titmuss, Richard.
1963 *Essays on the Welfare State,* 2nd ed. London: George Allen and Unwin.
Tobin, James.
1966 "The case for an income guarantee." *The Public Interest* 4 (Summer):31-41.
1967 "Children's allowances." *New Republic* (November 26):16-18.
Vadakin, James C.
1968a *Children, Poverty, and Family Allowances.* New York: Basic Books.
1968b "A critique of the guaranteed annual income." *The Public Interest* 11 (Spring): 53-66.
Waxman, Chaim (ed.).
1968 *Poverty: Power and Politics.* New York: Grosset & Dunlap.
Wilensky, Harold, and Charles LeBeaux.
1965 *Industrial Society and Social Welfare.* New York: Free Press.
Will, Robert E., and Harold Vatter (ed.).
1965 *Poverty in Affluence.* New York: Harcourt, Brace Jovanovich.
Winter, J. Alan (ed.).
1971 *The Poor.* Grand Rapids, Michigan: Eerdmans.
Zald, Meyer (ed.).
1965 *Social Welfare Institutions.* New York: Wiley.

6
How to organize
a field project

This chapter guides the forming, carrying out, and completing of a field project. Whether one works alone or with a group, he will follow the research steps outlined in Chapter 1, Section B. Chapter 6 follows the five steps and poses questions that must be answered if one is to move through a field project successfully.

The following questions are more than a record of a field project to help at the time of the final report or term paper. They do not ask just academic questions about the field project but confront crucial personal problems which must be dealt with. Although some questions may not be easy to answer, they help the researcher understand motivations and interests. Trying to find solutions will be a rewarding experience, even if there are no easy answers.

Each researcher's perspectives will be unique. The following outline should be used as a guide through a field project as well as a diary of personal and intellectual progress. This systematic approach should help make the project a rewarding and enjoyable experience, while providing a framework for the final written or oral report.

I. PROBLEM SELECTION

A. Choosing an interest area
  1. Select the bureaucracy which most interests you.
  2. Why do you choose this bureaucracy?
    a. personal reasons
    b. academic reasons
B. Choosing the problem area
  1. What aspect of this bureaucracy interests you?
  2. Why do you select it?
  3. Is your interest area the same as that of the other members of your group? If not, how will you reconcile differences?
C. Stating the problem
  1. State the basic problem. Develop its relationships to the bureaucracy you are considering.
  2. Is the problem manageable within the allotted time? If not, why not? How can you make it manageable?
  3. Outline the time each part of the problem will take.

D. Describing the problem
  1. What are its aspects or variables?
    a. aspects
    b. variables
      i. independent
      ii. dependent
  2. Why do you choose these aspects or variables as important? Explain your rationale.
  3. What is the relationship between the aspects and variables?
  4. What aspects or variables are not included that might have been? What extraneous variables must you watch out for?
  5. What are your biases in this project? How will you control them?

II. PROBLEM STATEMENT OR HYPOTHESIS

A. State your hypothesis in an "if-then" form. State your problem in a complete and careful way.
B. Describe why you state your hypothesis or problem as you do, and indicate its personal and intellectual significance.

III. DATA COLLECTION

A. Choosing among research techniques
  1. What research techniques are you considering?
  2. Why are you considering them? What data do these techniques provide that others will not?
B. Deciding on a research technique
  1. What is your choice of a research technique?
  2. Why did you make this choice?
  3. What data will this technique gather?
  4. What difficulties might you have with this technique? How would you overcome them?
C. Choosing between measures
  1. How will you use the techniques to gather data?
  2. How will you measure or count aspects or variables?
    a. aspects?
    b. variables?
      i. independent
      ii. dependent
  3. Are the procedures noted sufficient to get all necessary information?
D. Deciding on a measure
  1. How will you obtain the necessary information?
  2. Give details as to how you plan to measure each aspect and variable.

    3. Give details as to how you will measure data on additional points of interest.
    4. What are the advantages and disadvantages of the measures you have constructed?
    5. What problems did you have in constructing the measures, and why?
      a. technical
      b. intellectual
      c. personal
E. Selecting respondents
    1. What would be the ideal sample for testing your hypothesis or exploring your problem?
    2. Who will be your respondents?
    3. Why did you choose them?
    4. How many respondents do you need? Why?
    5. How representative are your respondents of the population or problem studied? Will this amount of representativeness affect your results? How?
    6. How will you contact respondents?
    7. What are some alternative approaches if you have difficulty obtaining respondents?
    8. What extraneous factors—sex, age, length of service—do you need to control? How will you control their influence?
F. Pre-testing
    1. How will you pre-test your measure?
    2. Who are the comparable respondents you will use for a pre-test?
    3. How large a pre-test is necessary?
    4. Did the pre-test give enough information to test the measure?
    5. Was your pre-test a success? Why?
    6. What changes must you make in your measure?
    7. Do these changes improve the measure?
    8. Do you need another pre-test? Why?
G. Administering the measure
    1. How will you administer the measure? What time limits do you have? What division of labor will you use?
    2. What happened when you administered the measure? Mention the problems and situations that developed and how they were treated.

IV. ANALYSIS

A. Analyzing the data
    1. How many sets of data do you have to analyze?
    2. How will you analyze them?
    3. What data have you collected about the aspects and variables studied?
      a. aspects
      b. variables

    4. What additional relevant data did you obtain?

    5. How will you interpret data on aspects of the problems or independent and dependent variables?

    6. How can these relationships be most clearly shown? Will you use tables, graphs, or summations of observations? Which alternative do you prefer? Why?

    7. Present your data.

B. Judging the hypothesis or exploring the problem

    1. Is your hypothesis supported? Do you now begin to understand the basis of your problem?

    2. What extraneous factors influenced your results?

    3. How could you have controlled these extraneous factors?

    4. What is your feeling about the hypothesis or problem and the data which test or explore it?

C. Interpreting results

    1. What were the greatest problems in the project? What could have been done about them?

    2. Did these problems affect your results?

    3. Should you have been able to foresee these problems?

    4. What is the relationship of the hypothesis or the problem to the project? Did it support or contradict your initial ideas?

    5. If you repeated this project, what changes would you make? Why?

    6. What contribution can you make to the general area you researched? Do you look at the previous studies differently now? Why?

    7. What is your personal feeling toward the area? Has it changed from your previous feeling?

    8. What have you learned that you did not know before?

    9. What have you learned about yourself and your relationships with others?

V. THE FINAL REPORT

There are no questions about this step because the final report is each person's responsibility. By this time the researcher should have an idea of where he has been and why he was there. The report revolves around the major steps of the research process, but the procedure is flexible. The researcher should consider the report's basic design, length, and what is omitted and included before proceeding to prepare the report. If the researcher has carried out a field project as a member of a group, there must be a decision on what each person will contribute. Other than these considerations, the researcher will present his final report in the way he thinks most appropriate to illustrate what has transpired. What is learned that is most important, and each person must evaluate his own knowledge and experience.

Appendix

A. THE USE OF SOCIOLOGICAL METHODOLOGY IN FIELD PROJECTS

1. The Importance of Sociological Methodology for Field Projects

The field project—its investigation of the empirical world to verify ideas held about that world—has been the emphasis of the previous chapters. The application of sociological methodology is necessary for data collection in the project.

Before outlining some methodologies, we need to consider basic issues in sociology. It is important to remind oneself of the "introductory" nature of field projects. Not attempts to collect systematic and exhaustive data on the subject in question, they use research techniques to have clearer access to dimensions of society otherwise not seen. Methodological sophistication is not necessary to be successful in a field project; all that is needed is imagination, interest, and guidance in crucial areas.

Beginning social scientists are more interested in how the world actually works than in the best way to study it logically. The orientation of the field project supplies aboundant access to these workings and also to logical, rational deduction. It is best to encourage creativity, tempering it with direction and modification when needed, and to recognize that failure, from a methodological standpoint, may be looked at from a different view as success of the highest order.

It is important to learn how logical abstraction can distort empirical reality (Stein and Vidich, 1963). One is traditionally exposed to abstract learning based on books, lectures, and class discussion, which describes life but is not the real thing. While we do not discredit this knowledge, we have found that the reality of an empirical situation can be lost when put into abstract form. We know that reading about an event or seeing it on television is not the same as attending the event; therefore we ask people to participate in a field project to take part in the actual situations shaping contemporary urban life. Experiencing a field project is participating in a social process. It attempts to eliminate the gap between the abstract and the empirical world. Spending a day or a week gathering information among people different from oneself is more illuminating than reading a book on a different lifestyle. While the book may be true, it is the experience that makes it alive and relevant and adjusts one's beliefs to the reality.

We are often unaware of the interrelatedness of things. Our cultural emphasis on rational, scientific, and mechanistic views of the world tends to make us see the world in segmented parts, and it is not unusual to think in mono-causational terms. For example, one might say the public welfare system is inadequate because it is run by rigid bureaucrats, and if we can eliminate rigid bureaucrats, all will be well. Inadequacies stem from more factors than rigid administrators, such as inadequate funds, poor communication between clients and bureaucracy, or lack of national commitment to welfare.

Monocausational interpretations can be misleading. Major problems in current social unrest result from people who, in their desire for social change, are not aware of the complexity of social situations. Ousting rigid administrators may be an unprofitable act, possibly destroying services to the clients in whose name the action is undertaken, as well as causing serious disruption to the structure of a relatively efficient bureaucracy. While the desire for change is legitimate, in pressing for specific changes, one must avoid being haphazard or destructive. Activists must acknowledge the interrelated nature of all social phenomena. Interest, effort and involvement over a period of time provide information from several perspectives.

Many urban problems have been heavily studied. The three bureaucracies we are interested in have been exposed often ruthlessly, and inevitably individuals and organizations have been injured by such exposure. This is not to deny that these studies have produced beneficial results, but we should be concerned about where the beneficial quality lies.

Researchers with field projects must consider the ethical and moral dimensions of their studies as well as the learning assets. Field projects are not designed to expose problems, which is the way that many bureaucracies and their clients now tend to interpret study of their activities. As tools for providing access to phenomena happening in the world, field projects are most beneficial when presented openly. It is not unusual to meet resistance in the areas one wishes to investigate. Only after reassurance about the real intent of the field project is permission received, and sometimes not even then. It is worthwhile to be honest and open in attempting to get permission to study, even outlining the project to the person. Hopefully a few successful field projects will assuage some of the ruffled edges while allowing honest investigations of crucial areas.

Problem selection is personally revealing, because our biases make us interested in one thing more than another. From the outset, this makes it a little difficult to give full consideration to other aspects which may be equally or more important than the phenomenon in question, and a distortion of the empirical situation as well as a value judgement may result.

Seeley (1963:59) says that "we. . .intervene against some 'bad guys' in favor of some 'good guys' but such intervention is done by our biases, by unacknowledged canons and. . .[by] no ordered, let alone explicit and shared principle." An example may clarify this statement. There have been many recent incidents of police overreaction. Because of mass media's interpretations of police actions, police have fallen into disfavor with some liberals. It is not uncommon for someone to choose to study the police who has an interest in documenting a preconception that all police are violent. This study could be undertaken with the hypothesis that police tend to be more authoritarian than others. If the data are in the predicted direction, one might conclude that police violence is a product of their authoritarian nature. Concluding without full consideration of the issue overlooks other variables contributing to the hypothesized relationship, such as social class, ethnicity, and religion. The summation is premature.

This type of inadequate research encourages people to dislike police and further activate the chain of reactions. The police withdraw farther and become more defensive, amplifying the common belief and thus working out another example of a self-fulfilling prophecy. Seeley (1963:61) suggests that social sciences do this all the time, usually unwittingly. Sociological studies have powerful effects. They are not "mere findings, but findings for and against, judgements as well as verdicts and, in their redefinitional effects, acts of legislation as well" (Seeley, 1963:59).

We should have some of these contingencies in mind when we research and conduct field projects. One needs to recognize preconceptions, and while we may not expect to have a clear perception of all the implications, we can expect some recognition of the problem, some behavioral and attitudinal change based on the recognition, and a minimum of distortion of empirical phenomena. By being aware of the issues of definition and content and the social constraints in which they occur, we term field projects experientially based learning.

2. Methodological Techniques Appropriate for Field Projects

The following descriptions of sociological methodologies give basic ideas and requirements. The reader is referred to entries in the bibliography for detailed explanations. Any one of the techniques is appropriate for field projects, but the researcher must remember that the experiential aspect of research is most important.

a. The interview

The interview is the most direct and comprehensive means of data collection, using a person-to-person situation with the researcher asking questions of the respondent. The immediacy of the interview situation allows the researcher to use either of two approaches: unfocused interview, in which the sequence of topics and questions to be discussed is not predetermined; and focused interview, in which responses are sought to specific predetermined questions. The former is useful in exploring a field or generate hypotheses; the latter is suitable when the researcher is attempting to gain data with which to accept or reject a tentative hypothesis.

The procedure followed within an interview is called the interview schedule. It refers to the standardized interview sequence established to ensure comparability of responses from one interview to the next. The interview schedule can be composed of many types of items; an effective item sequence for eliciting much information is to become increasingly focused, beginning with broad, open-ended questions, and becoming more specific, encouraging precise replies.

The interview technique is best suited to situations where opinions and attitudes are sought, where the responses are not easily precoded or anticipated. It is also a good technique to use when the respondent has limited literacy skills. But with all types of respondents, the great advantage of the interview is its ability to catch subtleties and nuances of feeling. The immediate, interactive nature of the interview controls against contamination of misunderstandings of the question or instructions, because the interviewer can clarify ambiguities.

The interview is an interactional situation. Inevitably aspects of human interaction processes intrude on the validity of the administration of the interview schedule. While the interviewer should strive for personal awareness and control of his affective reactions to the respondent, as these influence the respondent's answers, total control is impossible. Even if the interview is totally controlled verbally, there are nonverbal cues emitted to which the respondent reacts. Because it is closely based on interaction patterns, the interview technique is highly subject to reactivity through the operation of the social desirability response, distorting responses and lessening the validity of the results.

Another disadvantage of the interview is a practical one—it is costly in time and money. For this reason, the interview is best suited to small-scale studies requiring in-depth material.

b. The questionnaire

The most widely used research technique, the questionnaire is most appropriate when the researcher wants to determine how his respondents measure in certain areas. The format is a standard, uniform list of questions all relating to one another in measuring a facet of the topic under study.

A questionnaire is the best way to collect several kinds of factual information; marital status, sex, income, education, occupation, and religion are easily obtained. This is called face sheet data and is usually placed together, at either the beginning or the end of the questionnaire. Questionnaires are also useful in obtaining responses about opinions, behavior patterns, and understandings.

The questionnaire generates information from responses to items which together approximate an interview schedule. In order to get the desired information, the way in which questions are formulated and phrased must be carefully planned. Frequently many drafts are necessary to be fairly sure each item measures what the researcher intended. There are several guidelines for item formulation: The item must be related to the research hypothesis; the item format, open-ended or fixed-choice, must be appropriate to the specificity of the information sought; it must be clear, concise, and unambiguous; the item must not suggest the response; items seeking sensitive, personal information must be phrased in a nonjudgmental manner; and sensitive or embarassing information ought to be asked at the end of the questionnaire (Kerlinger, 1964:473-475). Before administering a questionnaire, the items have to be pre-tested or tried for coherence and meaning on respondents similar to those in the actual study. After pre-testing, the researcher may find that certain items can be omitted because they contribute no information; that other items may be separated into shorter, more specific components; and that some items need reformulation or rewording for better measurement of what is intended.

The questionnaire has many advantages. Because of its standardized form it can be given to large groups with relatively little cost of time or money. Standardization of items means that information received is ready for analysis; researchers can be fairly certain that all respondents received the same test stimuli because of the questionnaire's uniformity. The impersonality of the administration creates a feeling of anonymity which may result in greater honesty and frankness of responses.

While the greatest advantage of the questionnaire is its efficiency, there is the possibility that predetermined responses distort the actual responses. The respondent has to channel his own reality into the alternatives provided by the researcher, and the fit is often imperfect. Because of the impersonal nature of the method, the researcher has no way of knowing the respondent's frame of mind when answering the items or his perception of what they mean. Language skills, literacy, and conceptual ability intervene to distort responses. Repeated pre-tests control this influence and are a necessity in eliminating communication difficulties and multiple interpretations of items (Cicourel, 1964).

c. Participant observation

In some respects this technique is used in all field projects. Its most general meaning is synonymous with the generic research term *field work*. In this sense participant observation refers to the researcher's being a participant in the social process in which he is interested. We unknowingly use participant observation all the time in our daily activities, although this form differs from its research use. In daily life we are not trying to make systematic sense of observations; for example, collecting all our observations on family life to form a study of the same. Participant observation in its sociological sense attempts to do this, to make sense or meaningful interpretation of observed behavior patterns.

In using participant observation we select a topic, such as the behavior of junior high school students in class and going to and from school. We go where we can observe the behavior, getting permission for entrance and observation if necessary, and watch the behavior while recording our observations. The researcher can be more or less involved with the interaction he is observing. If he is analyzing urban gang behavior, he may be only able to get information if he is an actual member of that gang. A classic example of a study of this nature is William Foote Whyte's *Street Corner Society* (1955). On the other hand if the researcher is interested in the behavior of junior high school students, he may be able to get information by attending class and watching them go to and from school. It must be decided beforehand how much involvement is adequate for a particular field project.

Any field project can use participant observation. It can be the main technique of a project when an unusual opportunity is afforded, such as when someone has direct access to welfare workers or ghetto residents; and in other situations it can be a supplementary technique.

d. Test batteries

Test batteries have the advantage of being standardized; anyone using similar tests records the data in exactly the same way. Tests are regarded as having objectivity not found in other more subjective measures such as participant observation, open-ended questionnaires, and interviews. Tests fall into categories of intelligence and aptitude tests, achievement tests, personality measures and attitude and value scales. If one were interested in comparing the achievements of inner-city high school students and suburban high school students, he could use achievement and intelligence tests together with questions eliciting socio-economic information.

One must remember not to get carried away with the measurement aspect of tests. Although they provide hard data for evaluation, there is difficulty with interpretation. As explained in Part 1, a positive correlation between authoritarianism and violence does not mean that authoritarian personality characteristics are related to violent behavior. Social phenomena are much more complex than that. Other contingencies of using tests must also be considered. Assuming that a test exists that measures variables in which one is interested, what additional types of measurement should the researcher use to support his data? How long will his data analysis take? Is the time and effort needed to make such tests available, and is it worthwhile to spend it in this manner?

e. Use of documents

Some research problems may not require the researcher to obtain the data himself; he may be able to use previously collected and compiled information. Actual field experiences are not the only source of data. Many records and historical documents contain useful information for sociological research. The researcher's work could be assisted if he knew of available material and was able to integrate it into his research design. Easily available documents relevant for research include municipal budgets, voting results, local government statistics, census tabulations, libray circulation records, newspapers, newsletters of organizations, calls to the police, welfare applications, school enrollment, and hospital admissions.

Documents have several advantages for sociological research, "the low cost of acquiring a massive amount of pertinent data, . . .non-reactivity. . .[as it is] not unusual to find masking or sensitivity because the producer of the data knows he is being studied by some social scientist" (Webb et al., 1966:53). The influence, contamination, or distortion introduced by the researcher's influence on data collection is diminished because using documents allows analysis of readily available material. Documentary material is useful in exploring material, checking and testing hypotheses, and comparing the results of the data obtained. It is often available for large population segments and has been collected over long time periods, and longitudinal research and hypothesis testing are facilitated by measures for differing time periods. Changes in a neighborhood might be revealed by examining intra-agency statistics such as number and type of telephone calls to the police precinct, fluctuations in school enrollment, and variations in number and category of welfare applications at the welfare branch office. These statistics could supplement data from the census which may be several years out of date.

The researcher using documents needs to note carefully how and why the material was collected. Despite its extensiveness and thoroughness, document analysis remains secondary analysis or re-analysis. Those who collected and compiled the data operated within their own definitional boundaries which involved selectivity. The researcher using documents can do so with precision only if he recognizes and allows for the biases implicit in the material's original collection.

f. Content analysis

Usually content analysis is used as a supplementary data-collecting device. The reason is obvious from the nature of the technique; content analysis is not a research activity that immerses the researcher into the on-going interaction process. It organizes systematically different patterns in human communication; newspapers, books, radio, and recorded interviews. The analysis required takes place away from the empirical situation.

Content analysis involves selecting an interest area. One might be interested in the local Black Muslims' beliefs and their similarity to national Black Muslim ideology. One also has to select a communication form related to the interest area. Data about Black Muslims could be obtained by interview, questionnaire, or participant observation, but the ideology of the national movement can be obtained only from a content analysis of Black Muslim documents, the writings of the leaders, and information in the newsletter.

The researcher must set up categories for interpretation. In this example he would be interested in the typical themes that characterize the Black Muslim movement. He reads with the intention of recording major themes such as concern for Black nationalism and religiosity, and analyzes the frequency and tone of these themes. He must repeatedly read the material carefully and compare categories with one another for frequency and significance, which would then be compared with the beliefs of local Black Muslims gathered by more direct methods.

Content analysis is time consuming, and we recommend its use only when essential or relevant data can be gathered in no other way. Even in these cases it should be practiced on a relatively small sample so that more time can be spent on the field aspects of the field project. The method can be used to evaluate anything communicated: number and types of words found in textbooks with hostile references, speech patterns, and values, the latter (ideas held as good and desirable by a group) often being the object of content analysis.

g. Miscellaneous techniques

Sociological methodology is of many kinds and complexities. The techniques we have mentioned are those which have been utilized most successfully in field projects, the interview and the questionnaire being the most popular. Other methods have produced significant results, and it may be well to mention a few more here which may or may not give some additional ideas.

The sociometric technique gathers information on group patterns. The term *sociometrics* covers many scales measuring differences in social structures and processes, and is used by the researcher interested in the fairly obvious group patterns such as communication, interaction, and liking-disliking. Perceiving regularities requires the researcher to observe the group over time long enough to see patterns emerging and to systematically record these patterns as he sees them.

Another method of obtaining the same data is to ask group participants questions as to their perceptions of various communication and interaction patterns. Who is the most important person in the group? Who do you like best? Who would you most like to work with? There are ways to tabulate responses that allow interpretation of results. The sociogram, one means of tabulation, allows the researcher to see who receives most attention in a group, who the least, who initiates action. This method requires direct access to a group. A typical research question would be: Is the acknowledged group leader the actual functioning group leader, or who really holds the power in a specific type of situation?

Interaction process analysis is a form of sociometrics. It is an analytical device developed by Bales (1950) that sorts group interaction into twelve categories including solidarity, tension release, agreement, suggestion giving, and opinion giving. It is based on the idea that all group behavior has expressions in common. All groups have a task leader to see that work gets done and an emotional-expressive leader to hold the group together through loyalty, listening to problems, and being sympathetic.

These techniques are only a small number of the ones available. Some are suited to the limited time and complexity allowable in a field project; some not. Whatever the method, the researcher will have to consider time and complexity. He should remember that his primary task is to understand the interactional factors shaping our urban situation. These factors are real and can be seen. If the field project allows him to see them, then it fulfills its most important function. Too often social research reduces these factors to vague numbers and conceptual abstractions. While this type of research may be useful in professional capacities, it may often be the opposite of what a successful field project should be—concentration on the life forces of the modern community.

3. Supplementary Bibliography

Adorno, Theodor, et al.
    1950   *The Authoritarian Personality*. New York: Harper & Row.
Allport, Gordon, et al.
    1951   *The Study of Values: Manual of Directions*, rev. ed. Boston: Houghton Mifflin.

Bales, Robert F.
1950   *Interaction Process Analysis: A Method for the Study of Small Groups.* Reading, Mass.: Addison-Wesley.
Berelson, Bernard.
1952   *Content Analysis in Communication Research.* New York: Free Press.
Bruyn, Severyn T.
1966   *The Human Perspective in Sociology: The Methodology of Participant Observation.* Englewood Cliffs, N.J.: Prentice-Hall.
Campbell, Donald T., and Julian C. Stanley.
1963   *Experimental and Quasi-Experimental Designs for Research.* Skokie, Ill.: Rand McNally.
Cicourel, Aaron.
1964   *Method and Measurement in Sociology.* New York: Free Press.
DeCharms, R., and G. Moeller.
1962   "Values expressed in American children's readers 1800-1950." *Journal of Abnormal and Social Psychology* 44:136-142.
Edwards, Allen.
1958   *The Social Desirability Variables in Personality Assessment and Research.* New York: Holt, Rinehart & Winston.
Filstead, William J. (ed.).
1970   *Qualitative Methodology—First Hand Involvement with the Social World.* Chicago: Markham.
Glaser, Barney G., and Anselm L. Strauss.
1967   *The Discovery of Grounded Theory: Strategies for Qualitative Research.* Chicago: Aldine.
Goode, William, and Paul Hatt.
1952   *Methods in Social Research.* New York: McGraw-Hill.
Gronlund, N.
1959   *Sociometry in the Classroom.* New York: Harper & Row.
Hammond, Philip (ed.).
1964   *Sociologists at Work: The Craft of Social Research.* Garden City, N.Y.: Doubleday.
Hare, A. Paul, Edgar F. Borgatta, and Robert F. Bales (eds.).
1955   *Small Groups: Studied in Social Interaction.* New York: Knopf.
Jacobs, Glenn, (ed.).
1970   *The Participant Observer-Encounters with Social Reality.* New York: Braziller.
Kerlinger, Fred N.
1964   *Foundations of Behavioral Research.* New York: Holt, Rinehart & Winston.
Kounin, J., and P. Gump.
1961   "The comparative influence of punitive and nonpunitive teachers on children's concepts of school misconduct." *Journal of Educational Psychology* 52:44-49.
Levin, Jack, and James L. Spates.
1968   "Closed systems of behavior and the traditional family ideology." *Psychological Reports* 23 (3, Part 1):978.
Lindquist, E. (ed.).
1951   *Educational Measurement. Part 2.* Washington, D.C.: American Council on Education.
Lindzey, Gardner (ed.).
1954   *Handbook of Social Psychology*, vol. 1. Reading, Mass.: Addison-Wesley.
McCall, George J., and J. L. Simmons.
1969   *Issues in Participant Observant.* Reading, Mass.: Addison-Wesley.
Miller, Delbert C.
1964   *Handbook of Research Design and Social Measurement.* New York: McKay.

Mills, C. Wright.
    1961   *The Sociological Imagination.* New York: Grove.
Moreno, J., et al.
    1960   *The Sociometry Reader.* New York: Free Press.
Osgood, C., G. Suci, and P. Tannenbaum.
    1957   *The Measurement of Meaning.* Urbana, Ill.: University of Illinois Press.
Phillips, Bernard.
    1966   *Social Research: Strategy and Tactics.* New York: Macmillian.
Rokeach, Milton.
    1960   *The Open and Closed Mind.* New York: Basic Books.
Seeley, John.
    1963   "Social science, some probative problems," pp. 53-65 in Maurice Stein and
            Arthur Vidich (eds.), *Sociology on Trial.* New York: Grove.
Selltiz, Claire, et al.
    1959   *Research Methods in Social Relations.* New York: Holt, Rinehart & Winston.
Stein, Maurice and Arthur Vidich (eds.).
    1963   *Sociology on Trial.* New York: Grove.
Thurstone, L., and E. Chave.
    1929   *The Measurement of Attitude.* Chicago: University of Chicago Press.
Torgerson, W.
    1958   *Theory and Methods of Scaling.* New York: Wiley.
Warner, W. Lloyd, et al.
    1949   *Social Class in America.* Chicago: Science Research.
Webb, Eugene J., et al.
    1966   *Unobtrusive Measures: Non-Reactive Research in the Social Sciences.* Skokie,
            Ill.: Rand McNally.
Weiss, Carol.
    1966   "Interviewing low income respondents." *Welfare in Review* 4:1-9.
Whyte, William Foote.
    1955   *Street Corner Society.* Chicago: University of Chicago Press.

B. THE FIELD PROJECT IN A RURAL ENVIRONMENT

1. The Rural Environment

While many colleges and universities are located near urban centers, distance from urban areas does not mean that the issues discussed in *Social Change in Urban America* and this handbook disappear. On the contrary, it is our belief that urbanization is felt everywhere in our society. If this is so, the operation of the three public service bureaucracies in rural areas differs only in size and intensity.

In a rural area there is the sociological equivalent of the inner-city resident. He may be an Indian on a reservation, a poor black man, a poor white farmer, or just a poor person—all of which are structural counterparts of the inner-city resident. He is lower class, culturally underprivileged, and subject to the pressures of this lifestyle. He is at the bottom of the society's status ladder and will feel he is victimized. His conflicts with the society around him may not appear as dramatic and visible as those of an inner-city resident, but they are as deeply felt.

The rural resident may be on the opposite side of the ideological fence when it comes to many of the processes we seek to understand. The poor rural resident may find modern bureaucracies an intrusion on his lifestyle. If he is white, he may resent the attention given to blacks and Indians by the public welfare program, or he may dislike his children's studying subjects in school that are irrelevant. All these possibilities provide opportunities for field projects. The contingencies of the rural situation may foster field projects in which one can gather data not easily available in an urban setting.

There is no community today that does not have an equivalent of the three public service bureaucracies. All have a police force, educational facilities, and provision for public welfare. Although size and complexity may vary, the principles guiding their functioning are much the same. There are corresponding roles in rural areas that are analogous to those in urban settings.

The lack of complexity in the country is beneficial to field projects because the simplicity of the bureaucratic organizations highlights their processes. If a police force is staffed by four or five members, analysis of its structure and functioning is less detailed. One may get a better picture of the bureaucratic processes here than others who obtain glimpses of the mammoth bureaucracies in urban areas. Whatever the local manifestations of the public service bureaucracies, they are basic to the social processes shaping our lives.

Modern communication links rural and urban life. The all-pervasiveness of mass media was tragically revealed with the assassination of President John F. Kennedy, when it was estimated that 90 percent of the population knew of the shooting within an hour of its occurrence.

Field projects may be more salient in rural areas. The major difference from their urban counterparts lies in their foci. For example, movement of rural populations to urban centers continues to leave older people who either choose or are not able to move stranded in rural areas with few friends and little income.

Many have to go on public welfare. What happens to them? What happens to their homeland as it becomes increasingly unmanageable? Do they become public welfare recipients for the rest of their lives?

A similar situation prevails in education. Because of the drainage of manpower to urban centers, there are not enough qualified teachers in rural areas to meet the demands of specialized industrial life. How do the schools handle this problem? How do students react to it? Is the gap between what is taught in rural areas and what is needed for survival in the urban society getting smaller or wider?

Similarly, police in a rural community will not escape the current critical evaluation of their role made by the mass media. How do they perceive their role? How does the rural community perceive it? Has its perception changed? What differences exist between these perceptions and those found in the city?

The initial problem encountered in rural areas is an unawareness of how widespread industrial-technological forces are. In the city people are bombarded with reminders of who they are, where they are, and what is happening, while in rural areas the senses are bombarded less. Reminders of urban problems are irritations bothering one occasionally but which can be ignored most of the time.

The cities are beginning to realize that they have overlooked their problems too long. The problems are overwhelming and may become the same in rural areas. Though the typical rural bureaucracy and rural resident may appear less affected by urban society's problems, it is becoming more evident that their air and water is often as polluted as the air and water in the city, that towns are as poor financially as larger cities, and that their children receive inferior education. As people continue to become aware of urban areas' problems, we hope that the same awareness will appear in rural areas. We hope to provide some awareness of the scope of the problems concomitant with urbanization in rural areas as well as the city problems.

2. Examples of Rural Field Projects

a. The relationships of an Indian tribe to public service bureaucracies
The Problem   Three people were interested in the American Indian's plight. They visited an Indian tribe and investigated its relationship to the three public service bureaucracies of education, police, and public welfare.

The Hypothesis   The literature suggested that the Indians' situation would be very difficult. The researchers hypothesized that the Indian tribe's attitudes would be negative to the three bureaucracies.

Data Collection   Data collection consisted of interviews and participant observation. In the interviews they asked key members of the Indian tribe and bureaucratic officials their opinions of the public service bureaucracies. Data collection required the researchers to spend a week with the tribe and subsequent weekends interviewing representatives of the three bureaucracies about the tribe.

Analysis   Some aspects of the hypothesis were borne out and others were not. The Indians had negative attitudes towards police but did not have negative attitudes towards public welfare or schools, believing that the schools provided the key to bettering their social and economic positions. They neither approved nor disapproved of public welfare, but most were adamant in stating that they would never accept it. The researchers reached no consensus about the Indian tribe's attitudes toward the three public service bureaucracies.

They found officials in each bureaucracy who were pro-Indian and actually trying to help them, as well as officials obviously prejudiced against Indians, therefore the research produced mixed results.

b. A comparison of rural and urban attitudes toward future occupations

The Problem   Three persons compared graduating high school seniors' attitudes towards job possibilities in rural and urban areas.

The Hypothesis   The researchers believed the city high school seniors were more urbanized and wanted white collar and urban jobs, while expecting rural students to prefer to stay in rural areas doing traditional things such as farming, manual, and blue collar jobs.

Data Collection   A questionnaire was devised to ask the students, rural and urban, about their favorite school subjects, outside school interests, and work plans for after high school. Ten pupils were selected for each group.

Analysis   The hypothesis was supported among urban high school pupils, who selected as their favorites urban-oriented subjects and engaged in after-school activities of an urban nature. They unanimously wanted nonmanual, white collar jobs and to live in a large city.

The rural pupils wanted almost exactly the same thing. They mentioned urban-oriented courses as their favorites and were engaged in urban-type after-school activities. They wanted to settle in or near to a large city but did expect to have manual or blue collar jobs in the years after high school graduation. The results impressed the researchers because they indicated that urbanization has entered deeply into the typical American consciousness, even Americans in rural areas.

c. Rural police activities

The Problem   Five persons were interested in the daily activities of rural police. They looked at police activities on a typical weekend in three communities—a small town of 5,000 people, a hamlet of 600 people, and a rural area with 250 people scattered throughout a township.

The Hypothesis   They hypothesized that the more urban the community, the more sophisticated would be police techniques for handling daily activities. They expected the large community to be most sophisticated in police work, the hamlet second, and the township the least sophisticated.

Data Collection   To gather information the researchers formed into two groups and observed rural police. They planned to get information on ten topics from open-ended interviews and participant observation.

Analysis   Their hypothesis was supported for the town and the hamlet. The town had a ten-man police force and sophisticated methods of handling police duties, and the hamlet had a force of one full-time and one part-time man. The handling of daily activities was informal because with a small population the police knew everyone personally and dealt with problems with personal knowledge.

The township did not support expectations. It did not have a local police force because it was patrolled by state police. This difference in type of police made the daily routine in the township sophisticated. Not only did the state police have more to do—highway patrolling, relaying information to state head-quarters—but their methods were very modern. The state police cars and barracks had modern equipment, the officers took continuing refresher courses, and they were constantly training new officers which they said kept them up to date. The township did not fit the expected pattern.

d. Migrant workers and public service bureaucracies

The Problem   Four persons were interested in the contacts between public welfare agencies and migrant workers.

The Hypothesis   The literature suggested that migrant workers had difficulty with local public welfare agencies. A cause of difficulty was that workers felt they were entitled to welfare for the time they were not working because their annual income was within the boundaries established by the agency as poverty level. The migrant workers were not able to collect welfare because seasonal work demands numerous moves, and they were not able to establish residency in one area. The researchers hypothesized that migrant workers were unable to receive welfare benefits because they did not meet standards established without consideration of their circumstances.

Data Collection   Interviews and participant observation were the sources of data. The researchers examined migrant workers' outlooks and the local public welfare offices. They constructed their interview to measure how public welfare bureaucrats and migrant workers perceived the situation, how the situation was dealt with, the outcomes of these procedures, and what was done to alleviate the problem.

Analysis   The researchers found the problem to be more complicated than originally thought. They had difficulty communicating with migrant workers; many did not speak English well, and the few that did tended to be militant and most educated. The researchers were uncertain how this biased group would affect the study.

The researchers examining the public welfare bureaucracies found that there was no clear policy and that what had been done was inequitable. Some migrants received public welfare while others did not because they did not meet federal or state requirements. Residency was not as large an obstacle as anticipated; although important, it was the bureaucratic rules and regulations which prevented the migrants from receiving assistance. The project was complex and needed more study, but the researchers did believe the current situation was unequitable and in need of reform.

3. Suggestions for Rural Field Projects

a. A content analysis could be done of children's literature dealing with life in rural areas. How does this literature perceive the bureaucracies of public service, particularly police and schools? Are they considered in urban or rural perspectives?

b. An interview could be designed for junior and senior high school students in a rural area, asking them their perceptions of the public service bureaucracies. It might be hypothesized that the older the students, the more urbanized their perceptions of these agencies.

c. There are many communes of young people springing up in rural areas, most of them composed of urban refugees who have urban ideas they wish to undertake in a rural setting. There are conflicts between communes and the local schools, sometimes because communes wish to educate their children themselves or because the commune feels that what is offered in the local schools is not adequate.

d. One might compare the degree to which subjects such as art and drama are offered in rural and urban areas. It could be hypothesized that rural schools view these subjects as nonessential, whereas city schools view them as important to a complete education.

e. A questionnaire measuring general and specific values could be administered to rural and urban teachers to see the variation in the two groups' values.

f. A project might be designed to determine the goals of rural policemen, and through observation discover the effects such attitudes have on policemen's activities in their work.

g. An interview schedule could be developed to ask rural residents what they felt were the major strengths and weaknesses of their local police. This data could be compared with similar information collected from policemen about what they felt they should be doing.

h. Some people could spend time in a rural community to find out the political and economic issues and what effect they have on local police law enforcement.

i. Most rural areas have poor people from differing racial and ethnic backgrounds. A project could be designed to see what the attitudes of several of these groups are toward public welfare as a helping agency and as a way of life.

j. Many areas have food stamp programs for welfare recipients and low income people. A project could evaluate the successes and failures of such programs in several areas to find out why the results vary.

4. Supplementary Bibliography

Butwin, David.
    1968   "Portrait of a declining town." *Saturday Review* (October 5):17-19, 40, 42.
Fuchs, Estelle.
    1970   "Time to redeem an old promise: American Indian education." *Saturday Review* (January 14):54-57, 74-75.
Schrag, Peter.
    1968   "Appalachia: the forgotten land." *Saturday Review* (January 17):14-18.

Stein, Maurice.
    1960   *The Eclipse of Community.* Princeton: Princeton University Press.
Vidich, Arthur, and Joseph Bensman.
    1958   *Small Town in Mass Society: Class, Power, and Religion in a Rural Community.*
            Princeton: Princeton University Press.
West, James.
    1945   *Plainville U.S.A.* New York: Columbia University Press.

72 73 74 75 76   9 8 7 6 5 4 3 2 1